PHOTOGRAPHY DEPT
Hereward College
Bramston Crescent
COVENTRY
CV4 9SW

# 34

KT-447-804

ANNUAL EXHIBITION

# PHOTOGRAPHY AND ILLUSTRATION

COMMUNICATION ARTS

*Communication Arts (ISSN 0010-3519) is published eight times a year by Coyne & Blanchard, Inc., 410 Sherman Avenue, Palo Alto, California 94306*

*Copyright 1993 by Coyne & Blanchard, Inc.*

*Patrick Coyne, editor and designer; Jean A. Coyne, executive editor; Stephanie Steyer-Coyne, consulting editor and designer; Anne Telford, managing editor; Scott Perry, production manager; Ron Niewald, Scott Teaford, production; Michael Krigel, advertising and circulation director; Art Carbone, retail sales; Nancy Hagemann, administrative assistant; Sue Sprinkle, editorial assistant; Vickie Perry, subscription manager; Luz Hugo, Jason Jackson, Priscilla Solera, subscriptions; Lisa Marie Perez, traffic manager; Richard Coyne, founder*

002376

*This special issue is a combination of the* [illegible] *sues published exclusively for distribution by RotoVision SA, 9, Route Suisse, Ch-12* [illegible] *ax (022) 755 40 72, Telex 419 246 rovi ch.*

# INTRODUCTION

Welcome to the international edition of *Communication Arts*'s 34th annual Photography and Illustration Exhibition. The images on the following pages represent the finest examples of creativity in the service of commercial art for magazines, newspapers, books, advertising, posters, packaging and self-promotion.

Considered one of the most prestigious creative competitions in the world, we received over 16,000 entries this year. Our distinguished jury, comprised of respected creative professionals, selected 580 images for inclusion in this exclusive volume.

The competition is extremely important to photographers and illustrators because *Communication Arts* reproduces their work with an unprecedented level of quality and distributes this annual to 60,000 design and advertising professionals worldwide, guaranteeing important exposure for the winners.

This year's volume contains the work of many new artists who continue to expand creativity in photography and illustration with innovative approaches. Please enjoy this book as an invaluable reference to the current state-of-the-art in visual communications and as a statement of creative excellence.

# ご挨拶

このインターナショナル版には、「コミュニケーション・アーツ」主催第34回写真・イラストレーション・コンペティションの入賞作品が掲載されています。以下の作品は、雑誌、新聞、本、広告、ポスター、パッケージ、プロモーション用に制作されたコマーシャル・アートとして、卓越したクリエイティビティを象徴するものばかりです。

世界で最も権威あるクリエイティブ分野のコンペティションの一つとして、今回は16,000点以上の応募がありました。その中から、プロとして活躍中の著名な審査員により選ばれた580作品をご紹介します。

入賞作品は「コミュニケーション・アーツ」に最高のクオリティーで再現され、世界中の60,000人ものデザイン・広告関係者に紹介されます。受賞者にとってはまたとない機会となるわけで、このことからしても、このコンペティションは写真家、イラストレーターにとって大変に有意義なものといえます。

今年のインターナショナル版には、新しいアプローチやアーティストの数々が紹介され、写真とイラストレーションにおけるクリエイティビティの幅をさらに広げています。この本は、最新のビジュアル・コミュニケーションに関する参考資料として、また卓越したクリエイティビティの表現の場として、読者の皆様にとって貴重な一冊となることと思います。

# INTRODUCCIÓN

Bienvenido a la edición internacional de la 34ª exhibición anual de Fotografía e Ilustración de *Communication Arts*. Las siguientes páginas muestran las mejores imágenes producidas para revistas, periódicos, libros, publicidad, afiches, empaque y autopromoción, escogidas por su excelencia creativa en el servicio de las artes publicitarias.

Nuestro concurso de expresión creativa es considerado como uno de los de mayor prestigio en el mundo. Este año recibimos más de 16,000 muestras, de las cuales nuestro distinguido jurado, conformado por artistas profesionales de renombre, seleccionó 580 imágenes para incluir en este ejemplar exclusivo.

Este certamen es de suma importancia para fotógrafos e ilustradores dado que la revista *Communication Arts* reproduce sus obras de inigualable calidad y distribuye este libro entre 60,000 profesionistas de diseño y publicidad en el mundo entero, asegurando a los ganadores que sus obras se darán a conocer.

La edición de este año reúne las obras de artistas nuevos dedicados a la creación artística en el mundo de la fotografía y la ilustración. Lo invitamos a gozar de este libro que representa una referencia invaluable del estado actual de la comunicación visual, y un baluarte de la excelencia creativa.

PART ONE

# 34

# PHOTOGRAPHY ANNUAL

# CATEGORIES

# THE JURY

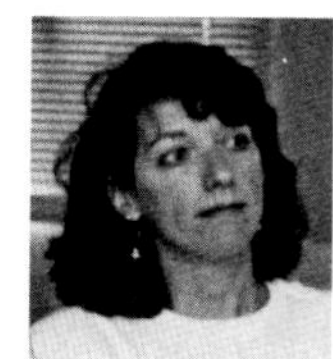

HENRY BRIMMER

came to the United States from Mexico to study agriculture at the University of California, Davis, in 1964, but filmmaking and photography diverted his attention from grain crops and cattle. For the next ten years he traveled through Europe, Africa, the Middle East and Asia. By some fluke he landed in Ulm, where he got involved with designers from the Fachhochschule fur Gestaltung (the New Bauhaus). He studied graphic design in Zurich and Essen and returned to the U.S. in 1978. Since then he has established his own design studio in San Francisco, has taught design at various institutions throughout the Bay Area and in 1982 launched *Photo Metro* magazine, a photography tabloid.

LAURIE KRATOCHVIL

first joined *Rolling Stone* as photography editor in 1978 after working at the *Los Angeles Times* and A&M Records. In 1980, she became photography editor of *New West* magazine and returned to New York and *Rolling Stone* in 1982. Under her direction, *Rolling Stone* has been nominated three times for the National Magazine Awards for photography and, in 1988, won this honor. In 1989, *Rolling Stone: The Photographs*, a twenty-year retrospective book that she produced and edited, appeared on the *New York Times* best seller list. That same year she was named director of photography, the title she currently holds.

LEONARD G. PHILLIPS

is a free-lance book designer and photographer in Charlottesville, Virginia. He was previously art director and photo editor for Thomasson-Grant, Inc. publisher of *Odyssey: The Art of Photography at National Geographic* and the American Society of Media Photographer's retrospective *10,000 Eyes*. Current projects include book design for the National Geographic Society, magazine photography and photography for a book on apple pomology. He received a BFA with honors from James Madison University.

LANA RIGSBY

is the principal of Rigsby Design, Inc. Based in Houston, the company specializes in corporate communications and identity development. Her work has been consistently recognized in major design competitions throughout the United States and includes numerous annual reports and projects that have been singled out for photographic excellence. Ms. Rigsby is a founding member and past officer of AIGA/Texas. Prior to establishing her firm, she was a principal at Lowell Williams Design for nearly ten years.

JEFF TERWILLIGER

is a senior art director at Carmichael Lynch, a Minneapolis-based advertising agency. Over the past four years he has worked on Rollerblade, Polaris, Blue Fox fishing tackle, Minnesota office of tourism and the Minnesota State Lottery. Work on these accounts has led to awards from The One Show, the New York Art Directors Club, the Andys and *Communication Arts*, in addition to being a three-time Stephen Kelly finalist. Terwilliger studied visual communication at both the University of Wyoming and the Minneapolis College of Art and Design.

## Advertising

1
Frank Herholdt, photographer
Lee Golding, art director
Miller & Leeves Waht, ad agency
Prestons, client

Ad headline: What's a girl to do if she can't find her diamond at Prestons?

2
Dennis Murphy, photographer
Armando Hernandez, art director
Tucker Hasler, writer
Bill Oakley, creative director
Temerlin McClain, ad agency
Dallas International Sports Commission, client

Billboard headline: See the wide world of sports without commercial interruptions.

3
Bryan F. Peterson, photographer
Chuck Pennington, art director
Ogilvy & Mather, ad agency
Nintendo, client

New game teaser. Ad headline: Only the animals know.

4
Terry Husebye, photographer/art director
Laura Tarrish, designer
Laura Tarrish Design, design firm
Primal Lite, Inc., client

String light manufacturer brochure.

1

2

3

4

1

2

3

## Advertising

1 (series)
Daniel Wreszin, photographer
Andy Frank/Daniel Wreszin, art directors
Andy Frank, designer
Jefferson/Acker, ad agency
Fostex Corporation of America, client

Ad headlines: My feet just, like, took over. They're already juiced when you show up. I can almost fit my whole studio in my mouth.

2
Brad Schwarm, photographer
Judy Little, art director
Riddell Advertising & Design, ad agency
Mongoose Bicycles, client

Ad headline over a double-page spread (left side is a copy page): The Thousand Words. The Picture.

3
Hans Neleman, photographer
Gabe Difiore, art director
Clockwork Apple, model maker
Eisaman, Johns & Laws, ad agency
Hiram Walker Inc., client

Ad headline: The colder the better.

4
Rick Rusing, photographer
John Boone, art director/designer
Team One Advertising, ad agency
Beechcraft-Starship, client

Magazine ad headline: You can tell a lot about a CEO by his wingtips.

4

## ADVERTISING

1 (series)
Robert Mizono, photographer
Rich Shiro/Dexter Fedor/Dennis McVey, art directors
Ketchum Advertising, ad agency
Bank of America, client

Ad headlines: A Unique Approach. The Right Balance. Structural Integrity. In a Different Light.

2 (series)
Håkan Ludwigsson, photographer
Morten Saether, art director
Reklambyrået Leo Burnett A/S, Oslo, ad agency
NSB Norwegian Railways, client

Ad headlines: The train is to let your thoughts fly. The train is a good book.

1

2

1

2

3

## Advertising

1
Nick Vedros, photographer
Tom Smith, art director/designer
Wyse Advertising, ad agency
Penton Publications, client

Ad promoting an article about the American economy, headline: Our Standard of Living is Dying.

2
John Huet, photographer
David Fox, art director
Wieden & Kennedy, ad agency
Nike, design/client

National apparel ad campaign. Headline: Machine Wash. Cold Water. Do Not Bleach. Tumble Dry. Have Heroes.

3
Bill Miles, photographer
Todd Riddle, art director
Hill, Holliday, Connors, Cosmopulos, Inc.,ad agency
Bank of Boston, client

Ad for investment portfolio which promotes an active lifestyle after 50. Headline: Every bank knows how to deal with a CD when it matures. But what about when the customer does?

1

2

## Advertising

1
Jim Arndt, photographer
Alan Godshall, art director
Stockton West Burkhart, ad agency
Ralston Purina Co., client

Ad for dog food. Headline: If you are going to hunt him under these conditions, you better feed him under these...

2
Jon Gipe, photographer
Hal Barber, art director
Terry Slaughter, creative director
SlaughterHanson Advertising, ad agency
Polarbek, client

Print ad for Village Management Apartments. Headline: Get a Life.

3
Stewart Charles Cohen, photographer
Jayne Bremec, art director
Grey Direct, ad agency
Sears, client

Direct mail selling children's lifestyles.

3

## Advertising

1
Glen Wexler, photographer
Hugh Syme, art director
Interscope Records, client

Album cover for Unruly Child.

2
Robert Lewis, photographer
Risa Zaitschek/Chris Austopchuk, art directors
Risa Zaitschek, designer
Sony Music Entertainment, design
Epic Records, client

CD cover, "Stanley, Son of Theodore: Yet Another Alternative Music Sampler."

3
Michael O'Brien, photographer
Susan Westre, art director
BBDO Los Angeles, ad agency
Apple Computer, Inc., client

Ad headline: PowerBook. It's the next thing.

1

2

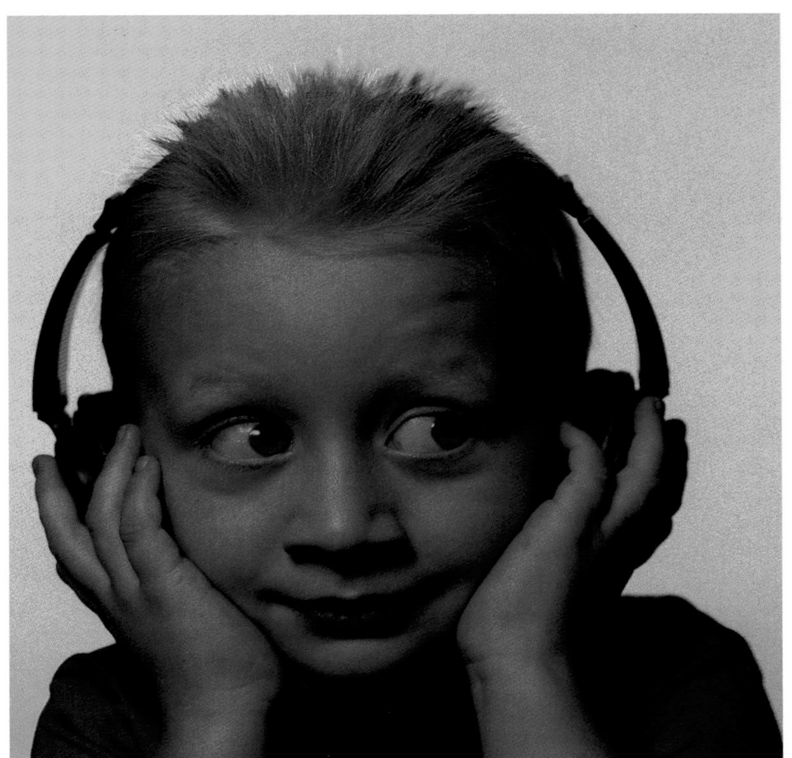

3

1

## Advertising

1 (series)
Robin Hood, photographer
Terri Burmester, art director
Bradley Communications, ad agency
Alaska Tourism, client

National print campaign. Headline for all the ads: 100 Pages of Free Advice For Anyone Ready to Discover Alaska.

1

2

## Advertising

1
Phil Banko, photographer
Mitch Craig/Mark Peterson, art directors
Pinnacle Effects, agency/client

Trade ad headline: Smashing special effects.

2 (series)
John Huet, photographer
David Fox, art director
Katy Tisch, designer
Wieden & Kennedy, ad agency
Nike, design/client

1
Malcolm Venville, photographer
Mark Denton/Andy McKay, art directors
Simons Palmer Denton Clemmow & Johnson, ad agency
Wrangler, client

2
Graham Westmoreland, photographer
Warren Eakins, art director/designer
Wieden & Kennedy, ad agency
Nike, client

Double-page ad to show how the shoes cope with difficult terrain. Headline: You might not be able to tell if the sky was 35% bluer today. But you'd definitely notice if your shoes had 35% more air. The new Air Max.

3
Sue Bennett, photographer
Bob Wisner, creative director
Hutchins/Young & Rubicam, ad agency
Eastman Kodak, client

Biker captured on Kodak High Speed Infrared Film.

4
Jeff Ott, photographer
Larry Johannes, creative director
Uniden America Corporation, agency/client

Used as a magazine ad, poster and billboard. Headline: Real pagers for a real world.

1

2

3

4

## Advertising

1 (series)
Nadav Kander, photographer
Mark Nightingale/Noel Hasson, art directors
Harari Page, ad agency
Mulberry, client

Headline: Mulberry handbags, an essential part of the English landscape. Head: The Gamekeeper's Bag; The International Grip; The Planner.

2
Frank Walsh, Rieder & Walsh, photographer
Brian Bronaugh, art director
Werner Chepelsky & Partners, ad agency
Mellon Bank, client

Billboard and bus card. Headline: There's always a new reason to preserve our neighborhoods.

1

1

2

3

## ADVERTISING

1
Bill Robbins, photographer
Steve Lauri, art director
Wakeman & DeForrest, ad agency
Upper Deck Trading Cards, client

Double-page spread, headline: Trade Up.

2
Jim Arndt, photographer
Arty Tan, art director
Fallon McElligott, ad agency
Icebox Custom Framing, client

3 (series)
Michael Lavine, photographer
Cliff Sloan, art director
The Sloan Design Group, design firm
Johnson & Johnson/MTV, clients

MTV's "House of Style" and Johnson & Johnson booklet used to show current trends and launch a new skin care product, Clean & Clear.

## Advertising

1
Joanne Dugan, photographer
Ann Lee Fuller, designer
Roth McMahon Communications, ad agency
Michael George, client

Direct mail card for a floral designer.

2 (series)
Clint Clemens, photographer
Warren Johnson, art director/designer
Carmichael Lynch, ad agency
Harley-Davidson, client

Running shots for literature, photographed in Milwaukee.

1

2

1

ORDER HERE
Fresh Squeezed ORANGE JUICE
PICK-UP
Fresh Squeezed LEMONADE
PICK-UP
1408

2

3

4

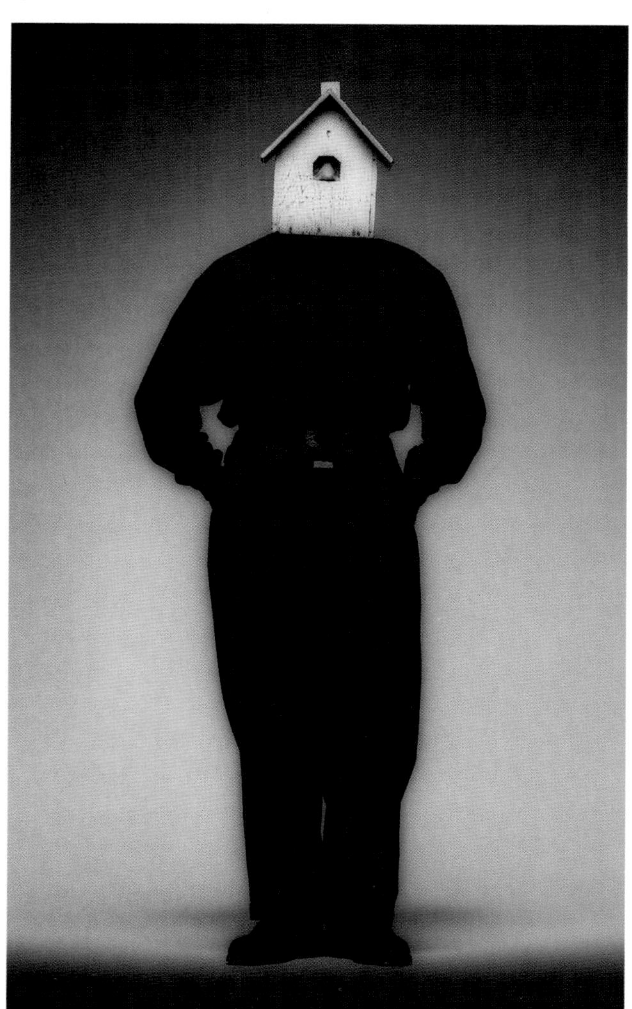

## Advertising

1
Stephen Wilkes, photographer
Oscar Recalde, art director
James Caporimo, creative director
Waring & LaRosa, ad agency
Perrier, client

Double-page ad headline: On a turnout along the Coast Highway just north of Laguna Beach there's a place where the talk is usually about water. They call it the Shake Shack. Perrier. Part of the local color.

2
Graham Westmoreland, photographer
Warren Eakins, art director/designer
Wieden & Kennedy, agency
Nike, client

Double-page ad for Air Huarache International. Headline: In a perfect world, it would never rain when you were out running. You'd also have a great fitting pair of shoes that didn't weigh much.

3
Lars Topelmann, photographer
Joe Shands/Mike Sheen, art directors/writers
Cole & Weber, ad agency
Klein, client

Ad headline: Make-up by Klein.

4
Tom Ryan, photographer
Melinda Jones, art director
Bartels & Company, ad agency
Piedmont High School, client

Poster for Leonard J. Waxdeck's Bird Calling Contest.

1

ADVERTISING

1 (series)
James Schnepf, photographer
Jacqueline Norris, art director
Home Box Office, Inc., client

Ad portraits from the HBO movie, *The Last of His Tribe*.

1

2

3

## Advertising

1
Brett Froomer, photographer
David Davidian, art director
Joel Sobelson, creative director
FCB/Leber Katz Partners, ad agency
Jamaica Tourist Board, client

Ad headline: Yes. Come to Jamaica and feel alright.

2
Brad Trent, photographer
Mike Schell, art director
Brian Mullaney, writer
Schell/Mullaney, ad agency
Computer Associates, client

Advertising campaign for Demo-Disc. Headline: Ping pong mania is sweeping the nation. Sales are bouncing through the roof. And my competition is swatting air.

3
Jim Erickson, photographer
Jelly Helm, art director
Larry Frey/Stacy Wall, writers
Wieden & Kennedy, ad agency
Nike, client

Ad headline: You cannot go back in time.

1

2

ADVERTISING

1
Wyatt McSpadden, photographer
Beverly Cook Perry, art director/designer
Graphic Design, design firm
Fiel Publications, client

Photograph for CD cover "Buck Ramsey: Rolling Uphill from Texas," a collection of cowboy songs.

2
John Huet, photographer
Tyler Smith, art director/designer/design firm
Louis, Boston, client

Spring apparel campaign.

3
Tom Ryan, photographer
Bryan Burlison, art director/designer
RBMM, design firm
The Richards Group, ad agency
Optique International Eyewear, client

Ad headline: Poor vision is no excuse for picking out an ugly pair of glasses.

3

1

## Advertising

1 (series)
Dominique Malaterre, Tilt Inc., photographer
Louise Marois, designer
Lumbago, design firm
Eclectic Hair Atelier, client

Magazine ads.

## Books

2 (series)
Kent Barker, photographer
Brian Nadurak, designer
Karin Pritikin, writer
Krause Nadurak Eickmeyer, design firm
Chronicle Books, client

*The King & I*, a little gallery of Elvis impersonators.

2

1

2

## Books

1
Fred Woodward, photographer
Patti O'Brien, fashion director
Jim Wageman, designer
Stewart, Tabori & Chang, publisher
Arts Counsel, client

Interior photograph from *The Color of Fashion.*

2
Pete McArthur, photographer
Stephen Doyle, art director/designer
Drenttel Doyle Partners, design firm
Harper Collins, client

Book cover for math study guide *Finite Mathematics.*

3
Jon Fisher, photographer
Jennifer Barry, designer
Peter C. Jones, picture editor
CollinsPublishers San Francisco, client

Interior photograph from *Black & White Dogs.*

3

## Books

1 (series)
Jeff Sedlik, photographer
Bonnie Smetts, designer
Lee Tanner, photo editor
Pomegranate Artbooks, publisher

Book cover and interior from *Dizzy: John Birks Gillespie in his 75th Year*. These photographs, from Dizzy's last photo session, were also featured in *Jazziz* magazine.

1

1

## Books

1 (series)
Howard Schatz, photographer
Howard Schatz/Bonnie Smetts, designers
Pomegranate Artbooks, publisher

Interior photographs from *Seeing Red: The Rapture of Redheads.*

1

## Books

1 (series)
Joel Grimes, photographer/ art director
Nancy V. Rice, designer
Wilson/Johnson Creative, Inc., design firm
Westcliffe Publishers, Inc., client

Photographs from *Navajo: Portrait of a Nation.*

1
Geof Kern, photographer
Deborah Needleman, photo editor
Richard Baker, designer
Washington Post Magazine, client

Professor Glenn Pfau instructs students on exactly what it takes to be a successful executive today. Thin soles and analog watches required, "Executive Grooming 101."

2
Scott Sharpe, photographer
The News & Observer, client

Newspaper article on the people and conditions in Haiti, "The Haiti You'll Never See."

3
Nicholas DeVore III, Photographers/Aspen, photographer
Bert Fox, art director/designer
Philadelphia Inquirer Magazine, client

Sunday newspaper magazine article excerpt from *Flesh & Blood: Photographers' Images of Their Own Families*, published by Picture Project.

4
David G. Toerge, photographer
West County Times, client

Stand alone feature. A worker for The Cirque de Soleil climbs a rope after washing down the tent.

1

2

3

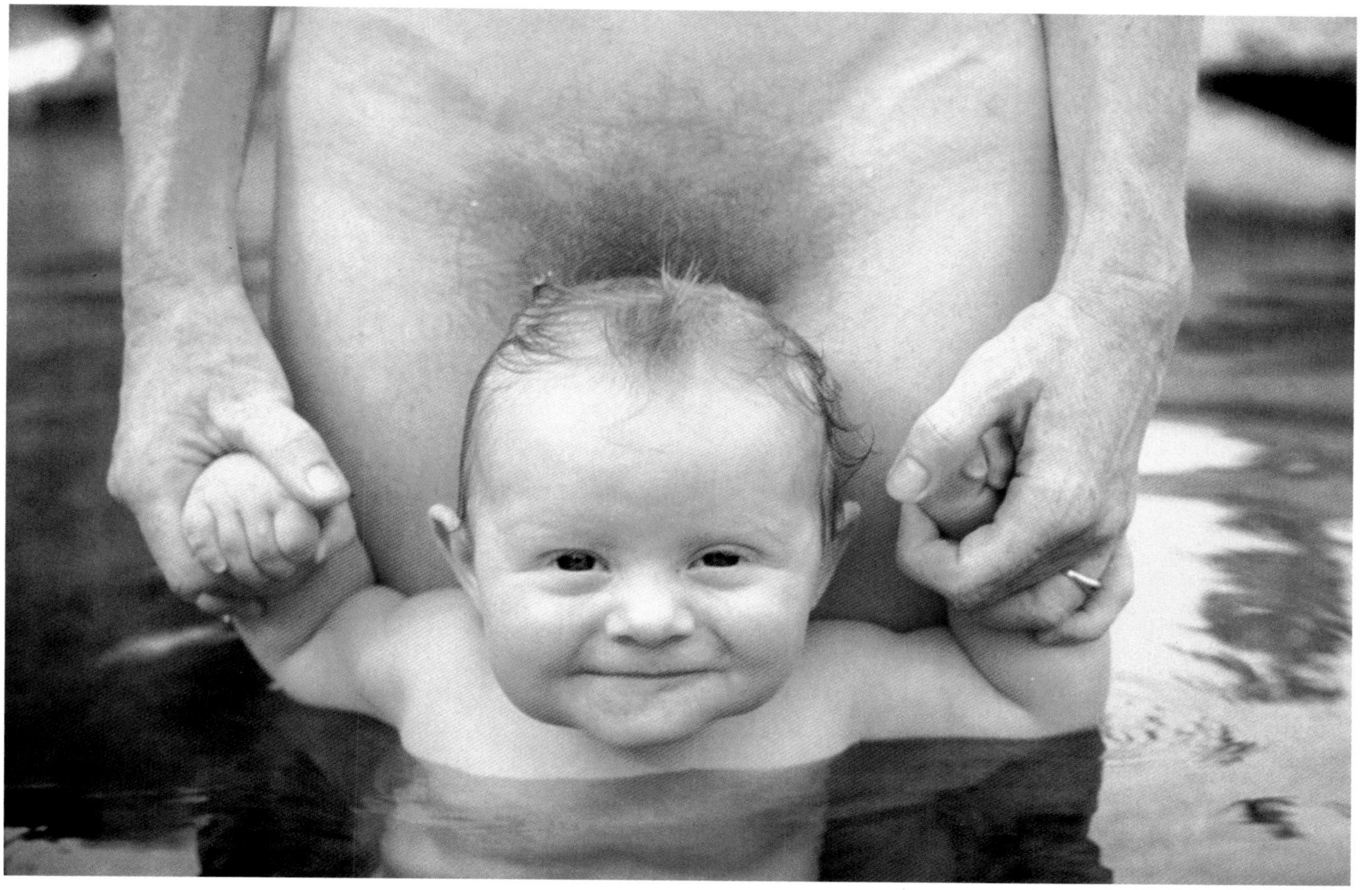

4

1

## EDITORIAL

1 (series)
Robert Holland, photographer
Erin Kenney Becker, art director/designer
Motorboating & Sailing, client

Magazine article, "The Agony of Andrew," illustrated the impact Hurricane Andrew had on the coastal Miami community.

2
Keri Pickett, photographer
Nancy Jo Johnson, photo researcher
Life, client

Photograph of the Blakeys, a Minneapolis family, illustrating a collector's edition magazine section, "The American Family, There is No Normal."

2

1

2

## Editorial

1
Max-Aguillera Hellweg, photographer
David Armario, art director
David Armario/Cathleen Munisteri, designers
Discover, client

Magazine article, "A Reasonable Sleep." Evolution suggests that if we sleep with our babies, we might help some of them escape sudden infant death syndrome.

2 (series)
Raymond Meeks, photographer
Matthew Drace, art director/designer
Men's Journal, Straight Arrow Publishing, client

Magazine photo essay, "Victory," the Northern Cheyenne tribal celebration for newly elected Senator Ben Nighthorse Campbell.

1

## Editorial

1
Chriss Wade, photographer
Victoria Seebeck, art director
Doug Renfro, designer
Whittle Communications, Special Report, client

Photo essay of human osculation, "Kisses Tell." Portrait of transvestite Michael/Michelle.

2
Geoffrey Clifford, photographer
Kate Patterson, director of photography
The Army Times Publishing Company, client

Jungle training school in Panama.

3
David Burnett, Contact Press Images, photographer
Michael Rand, art director
London Sunday Times Magazine, client

A young Navajo girl awaits customers at Monument Valley, Utah, "Shooting the Neutron Breeze."

4
Gianni Giansanti, photographer
Time, client

A starving Somali baby tries to get milk from his mother's shriveled breast, "Landscape of Death."

2

3

4

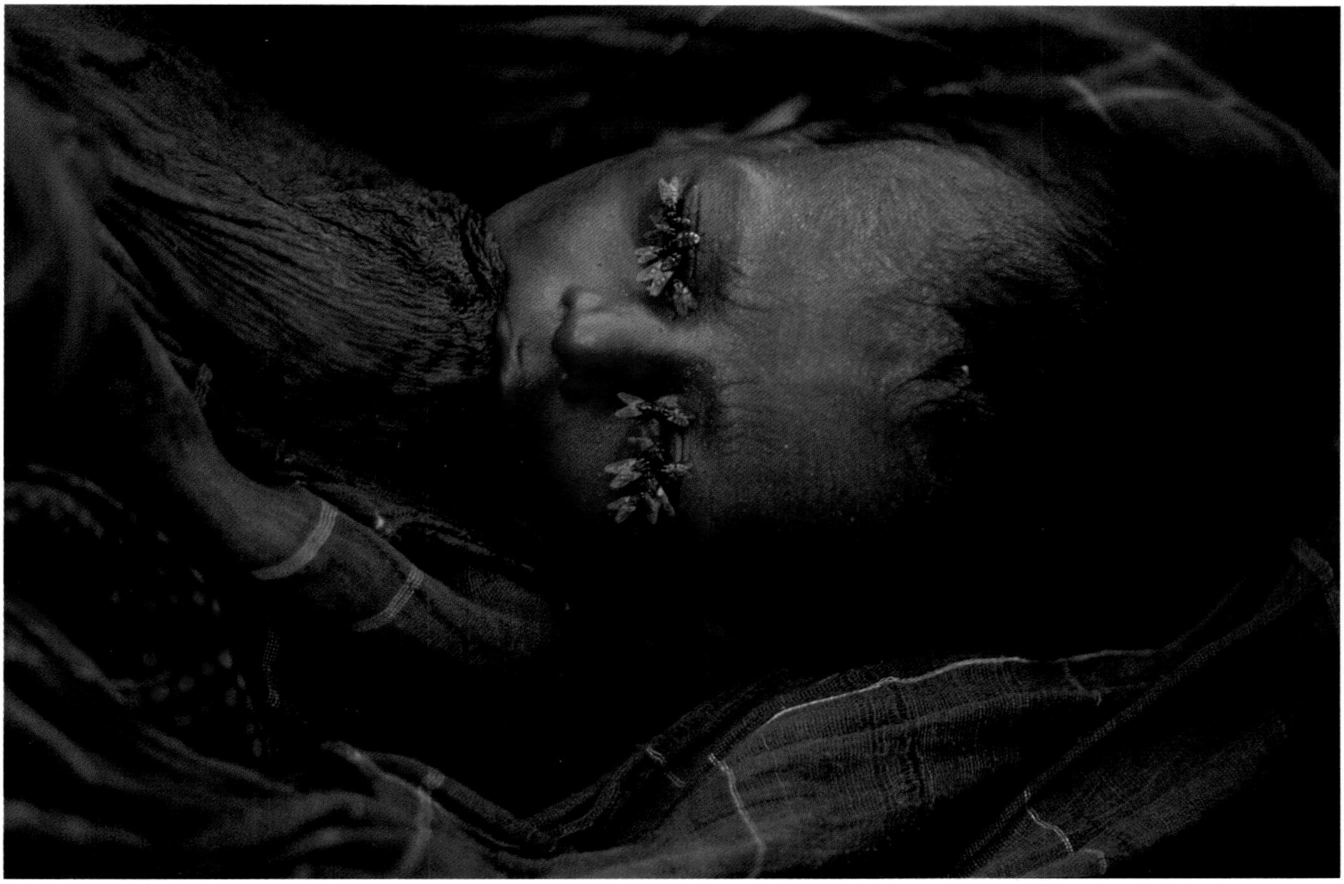

## Editorial

1 (series)
Bob Krist, photographer
Lou DiLorenzo, art director
Bill Black, director of photography
Travel Holiday, client

Views of the tea terraces on a plantation in Malaysia.

1

1

2

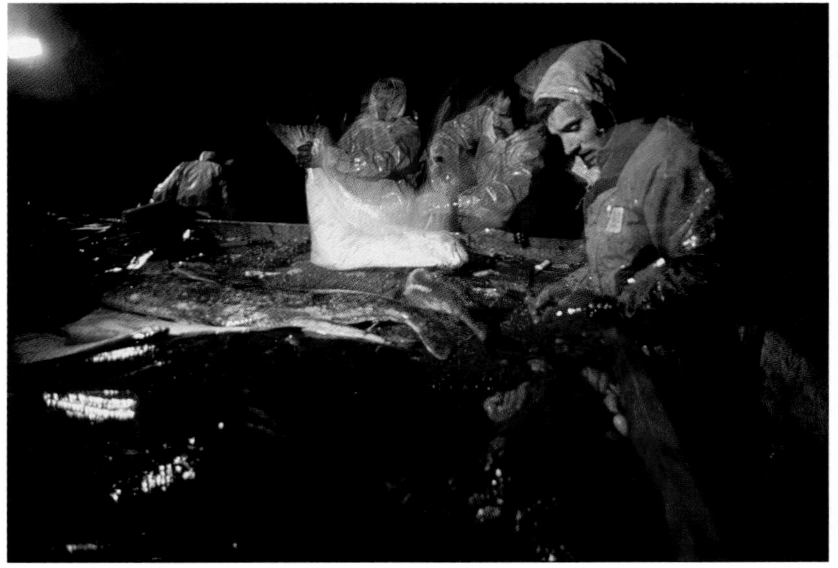

## Editorial

1
Mary Ellen Mark, photographer
Nancy Duckworth, art director
Lisa Thackaberry, photo editor
Los Angeles Times Magazine, client

In the flash of a luckless encounter, a sheltered Eagle Scout became both victim and killer in a chillingly brutal crime. Newspaper article, "The Good Boy."

2 (series)
Bob Sacha, photographer
Suzanne Morin, art director
Peter Howe, director of photography
Michael Robbins, editor
Audubon, client

Magazine article, "Alaska's Bloody Derby." A 24-hour season for Pacific Halibut, the Derby is a grotesque creation of modern fisheries policy that often threatens the lives of men and women who must fit a half-year's fishing into a single day.

1

## Editorial

1 (series)
Jiashu Xu, photographer
Nelphen Yung, art director/designer
Catherine Whitfield, photo editor
Emphasis (HK) Ltd., design firm
Mandarin Oriental Hotel Group, client

Hotel magazine *Mandarin Oriental*. Meditative moments among the Tibetans of Gansu Province.

1

2

3

## Editorial

1
Steve Payne, photographer
Michael Gregg, art director
The Globe and Mail, client

Book review of *Looking Around, A Journey Through Architecture.*

2
Nadav Kander, photographer/art director
Condé Nast Traveler, client

Photograph of a hydro power plant in Iceland, "Blue Lagoon."

3
Heidi Kirsten Wells, photographer/art director
The New England Journal of Public Policy, client

Photograph to illustrate the human element of homelessness and raise both money and awareness.

4
Tim Peters, photographer
Micca Hutchins, art director/designer
Sailing, client

Photo used as a double-page spread to highlight magazine selections of the best marine photography.

4

## Editorial

1 (series)
Mark Seliger, photographer
Fred Woodward, art director
Gail Anderson/Debra Bishop/Catherine Gilmore-Barnes/Angela Skouras/Geraldine Hessler, designers
Laurie Kratochvil, photography editor
Rolling Stone, client

Portraits of musicians Johnny Cash, Carlos Santana, Ringo Starr and Fleetwood Mac members Mick Fleetwood and John McVie for the magazine's 25th anniversary issue.

1

## Editorial

1 (series)
Dennis Marsico, photographer
Lou DiLorenzo, art director
Bill Black, director of photography
Travel Holiday, client

Places in the United States called Paradise.

2
David Burnett, photographer
Rudy Hogland, art director
Time, client

Magazine article. Chinese woman diver, Fu Ming Xia, wins the gold at the Olympics in Barcelona, "The Win-Win Games."

3
Bob Krist, photographer
Bob Ciano, art director
Hazel Hammond, photo editor
Ila Stanger, editor
Travel & Leisure, client

Article about Wrynose Fell, a highland area in England's Lake District.

1

2

3

Editorial

1 (series)
Mary Ellen Mark, photographer
Fred Woodward, art director
Gail Anderson, designer
Laurie Kratochvil, photography editor
Rolling Stone, client

Magazine article, "The Prince of Wildwood." Jack Brian searches the Jersey shore for love, girls and the future.

2
Danny Turner, photographer
Alisann Marshall, designer
Kyle Dreier, designer
American Way, design
American Airlines, client

Portrait of Super Barrio Gomez, defender of the poor. An ex-wrestler, he is now a champion of the poor and homeless in Mexico City.

1

2

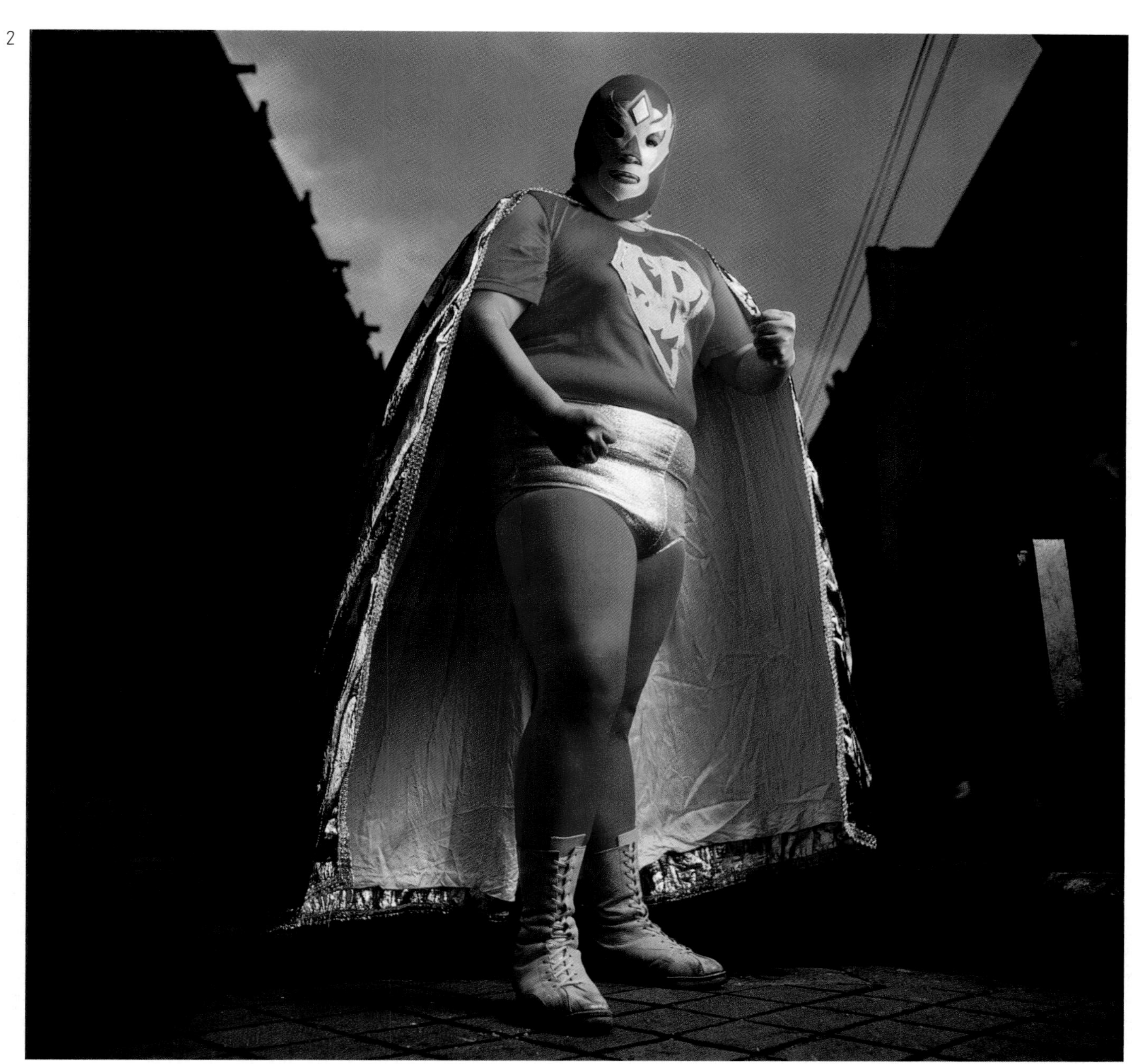

1

2

## Editorial

1 (series)
Dennis Carlyle Darling, photographer
Alisann Marshall, art director
Deb Miner, designer
American Way, design
American Airlines, client

In-flight magazine article on the Twinsburg, Ohio, convention for twins.

2
Pete McArthur, photographer
Giovanni Russo, art director
Men's Journal, Straight Arrow, client

Magazine article on Don Matao cigars.

3
Brian Smale, photographer
Robert Priest, art director
Karen Frank, photo editor
Gentlemen's Quarterly, client

Portrait of former Los Angeles gangster, T-Rogers, the original leader of the Bloods, "Original Gangster."

4
Jan Staller, photographer
Lou DiLorenzo, art director
Bill Black, director of photography
Travel Holiday, client

Night view of Niagara Falls.

3

4

## Editorial

1
Christopher Springmann, photographer
Susanne Rolf, art director/designer
IAPC, International Associates Publishers & Consultants AB, contract publisher
AGA AB, design/client

An interview with venture capitalist, William Edwards, in *Innova*, a magazine published for customers of AGA AB, an international industrial gas company.

2 (series)
Sacha Hartgers, Focus/Matrix, photographer
Bert Fox, art director/designer
Philadelphia Inquirer, client

Sunday newspaper magazine article, "Keeping Hate Alive." These German patriots are waving the flag of violence.

1

2

1

2

## Editorial

1 (series)
Alastair Thain, photographer
Mary Dunn, photography director
Doris Brautigan, picture editor
Entertainment Weekly, client

Cover story about actor Jack Nicholson, "King Leer."

2
Matt Mahurin, photographer
Jane Palecek, art director/designer
Health, client

Article about pathological liars, "The Great Pretenders."

3
Farrell Grehan, photographer
Alisann Marshall, art director
Kyle Dreier, designer
Doug Crichton, editor
American Way, design
American Airlines, client

In-flight magazine article, "Traces of Paradise," showing a present day Caribbean that comes close to when Columbus put ashore in 1492.

3

1

2

# Editorial

1
Amos Nachoum, photographer
Janice Van Mechelen, art director
Scuba Diving, client

Magazine cover photograph without computer enhancement.

2 (series)
Danny Turner, photographer
D.J. Stout, art director/designer
Texas Monthly, client

Magazine article, "Hooray for Big Hair." From Farrah to Ann, Texas women have combed, curled, teased and touseled their way into the national consciousness.

EDITORIAL

1
Edward Gajdel, photographer
Mary Dunn, photography director
Michele Romero, assistant picture editor
Entertainment Weekly, client

Portrait of singer Leonard Cohen, "Seven Reasons Why Leonard Cohen is the Next Best Thing to God."

2 (series)
Dennis Marsico, photographer
Lou DiLorenzo, art director
Bill Black, director of photography
Travel Holiday, client

Article on winter in Tuscany, Italy.

1

2

1

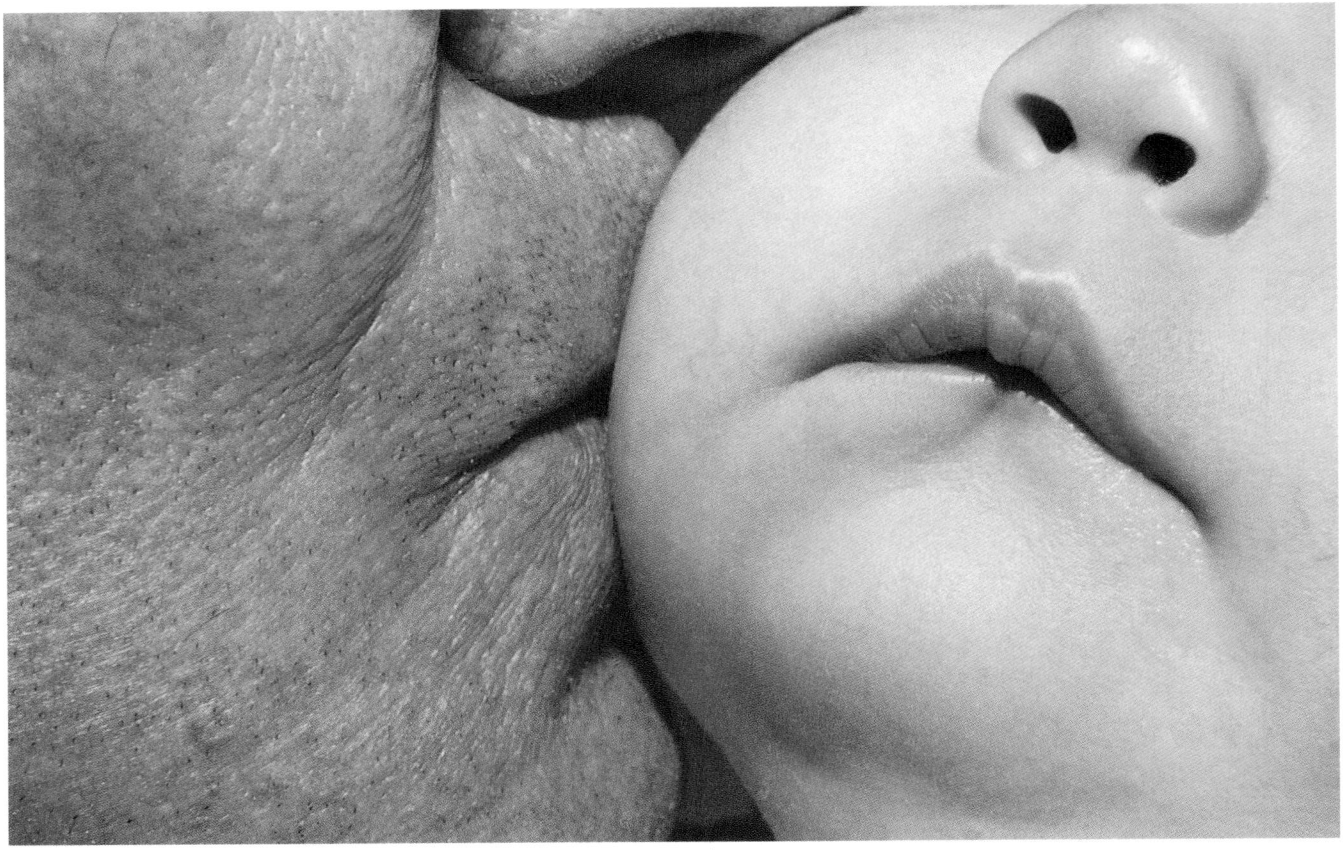

2

3

## Editorial

1
Robert Holmgren, photographer
Dian-Aziza Ooka, art director
Allyson Appen, designer
Tripp Mikich, photo editor
Parenting, client

Magazine article, "Are You Dad Enough?"

2
Robb Kendrick, photographer
Kathy Moran, picture editor
Tom Kennedy, director of photography
Bill Graves, editor
National Geographic, client

The reincarnated Lama in Nepal, "Gatekeepers of the Himalayas."

3
Chris Shinn, photographer
Donna Bonavita, designer
KPMG Peat Marwick, design/client

Portrait of a client used in a company magazine.

4
Richard Bickel, photographer
Lou DiLorenzo, art director
Bill Black, director of photography
Travel Holiday, client

Surfer from Salvador da Bahia, "Bahia Beat."

4

1

2

3

## Editorial

1
Lonnie Duka, photographer

From a *Communication Arts* profile of the photographer, showing his son Daniel.

2
Zbigniew Bzdak, photographer
W. Allan Royce, art director
Tom Kennedy, director of photography
National Geographic, client

Roaring through the earth's deepest canyon, risking their lives, a team of kayakers and rafters ride an adrenaline high down the seething fury of Peru's Colca River.

3
Mark Seliger, photographer
Mark Ulriksen, art director
San Francisco Focus, client

Portrait of Bill Moyers.

4
Charles O'Rear, photographer
David Arnold, illustration editor
Bill Marr, designer
National Geographic, client

"Bacteria. Teaching Old Bugs New Tricks." Aerial photo of salt ponds in San Francisco Bay illustrates colors created from bacteria.

4

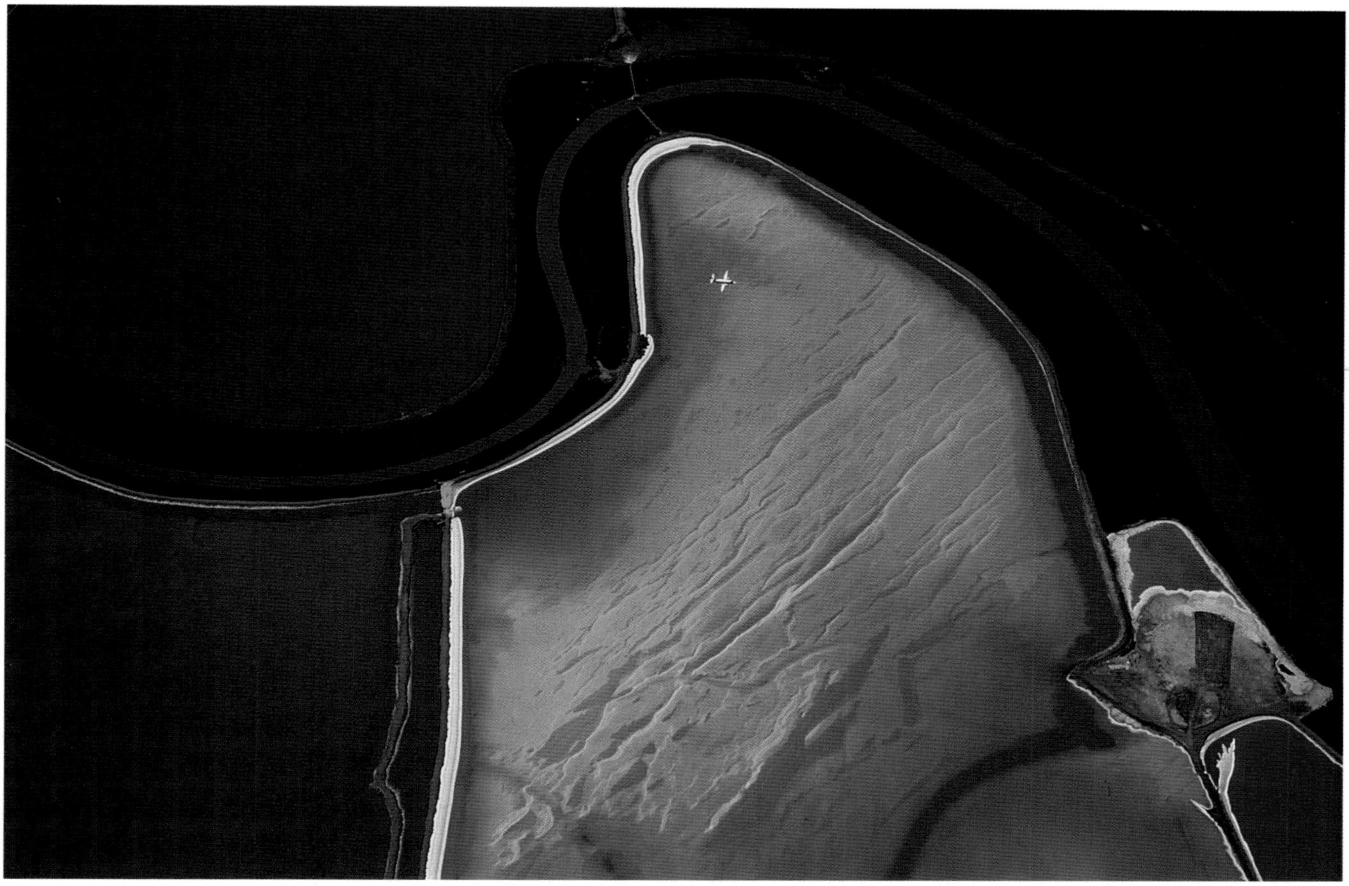

## Editorial

1
Pam Francis, photographer
Audrey Satterwhite, art director
The Houston Press, client

"A Man for All Seasons." Weatherman Dr. Neil Frank, an expert on hurricanes, appeared on the cover of the weekly newspaper shortly after the disaster of hurricane Andrew.

2
Dan Winters, photographer
Mary Dunn, photography director
George Pitts, assistant picture editor
Entertainment Weekly, client

Portrait of singer Matthew Sweet, "Body Bits: Face in the Mirror."

## For Sale

3
Ed Nielsen, photographer/art director/designer

Christmas card.

4
William Lesch, Swanstock, photographer
Verity Freeburn, art director
Etherton Stern Gallery, client

Poster.

1

2

3

4

## For Sale

1 (series)
Robb Kendrick, photographer
Butera's Restaurant, client

Prints for a restaurant display and for sale.

1

1

## For Sale

1 (series)
Vic Huber, photographer/art director
Tim Meraz, designer
Tim Meraz Design, design firm
Alfa Romeo of North America, client

The 1993 calendar printed by Dot Printer.

1

2

3 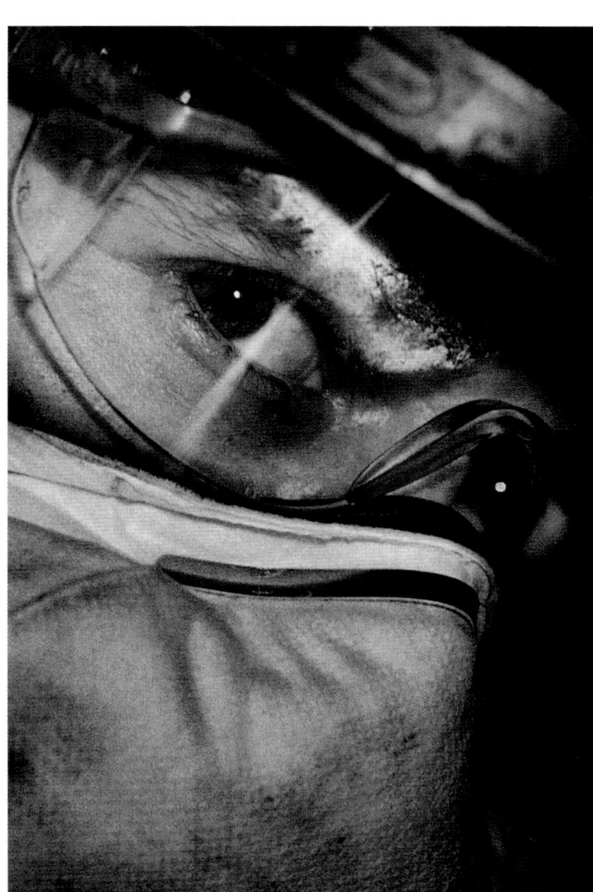

## For Sale

1
Burt Jones/Maurine Shimlock, photographers
Michael Bowmer, art director
The Art Group, Ltd., design firm
The Art Group Nature Collection, client

Secret sea visions poster of anemone in the Red Sea.

2
Felix Rigau, photographer

Trees and fog in San Francisco. Part of a project on designs in nature, sold as fine art.

## Institutional

3
Chris Shinn, photographer
Lana Rigsby, designer
Rigsby Design, Inc.,design firm
Serv-Tech, client

Portrait of a worker used on the cover of a facilities brochure.

4
Thomas Heinser, photographer
Thomas Heinser/Madeleine Corson, art directors
Madeleine Corson Design, design firm
Advertising Photographers of America, client

Auction poster for a Big Brothers/Big Sisters benefit at the San Francisco Museum of Fine Art.

4 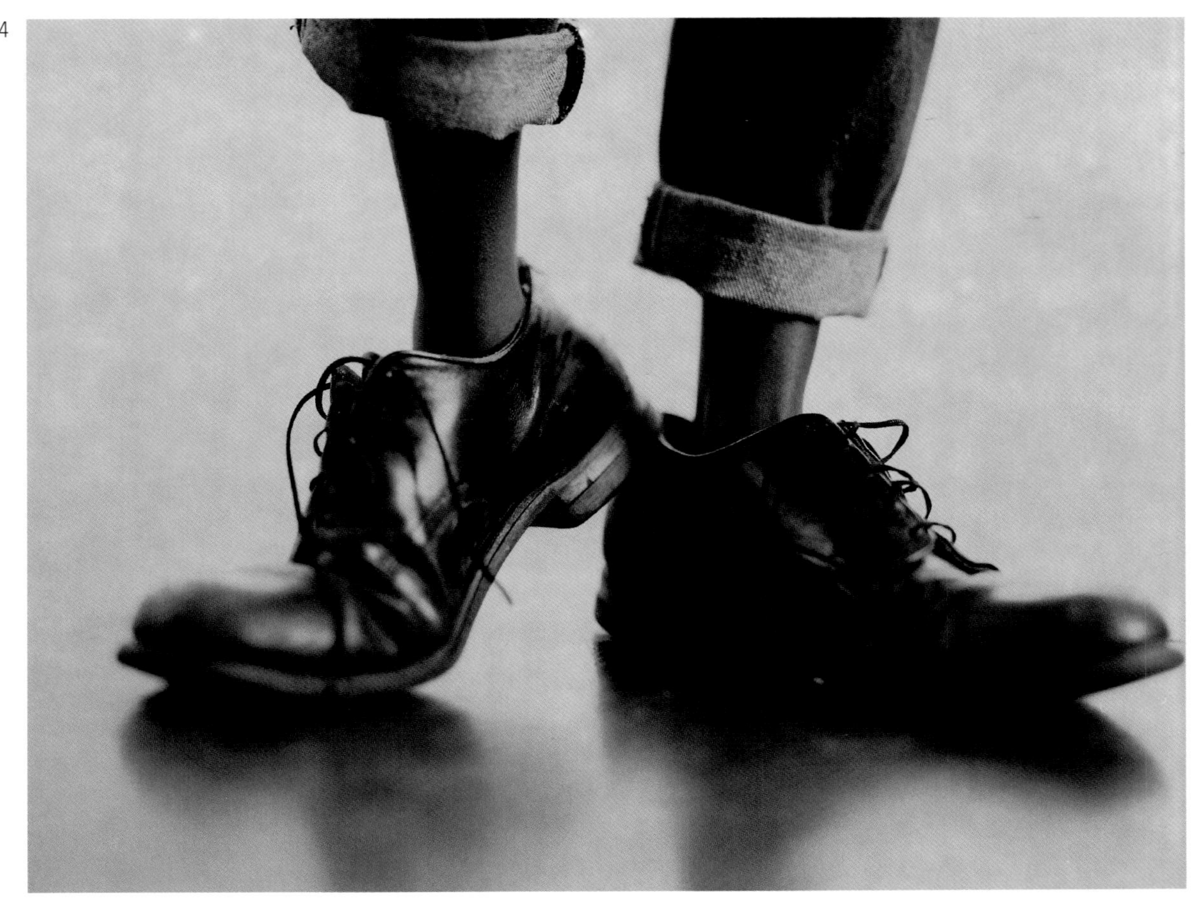

1

## Institutional

1
Scott C. Schulman, photographer
Chip Kidd, art director/designer
Alfred A. Knopf, Inc., publisher

Borzoi Books spring catalog cover.

2
Vernon Doucette, photographer
Russ Chapman, art director
Envision, design firm
Eastern Utilities, Inc., client

Corporate slide.

3 (series)
Marc Hauser, photographer
Gene Silverberg, Bigsby & Kruthers, art director
Jeff Nichols, designer
McDonald Davis & Associates, ad agency
Bigsby & Kruthers, client

Booklet showing notable Chicago personalities wearing the store's designer clothes: Lesley Visser, Michael Jordan and Phil Jackson.

2

3

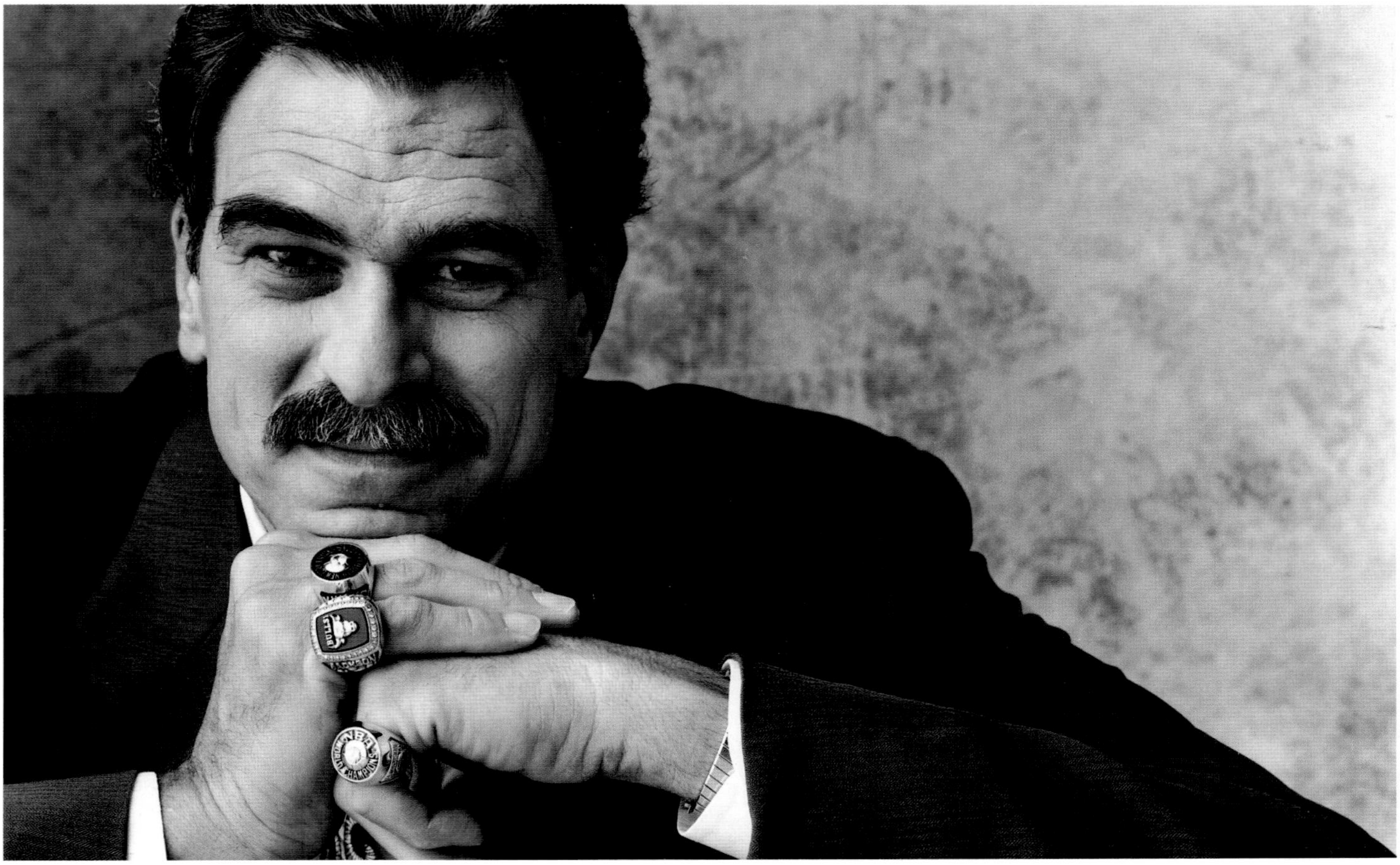

1

2

3

## INSTITUTIONAL

1
Steve Niedorf, photographer
Art Penfield, art director/designer
Mona Meyer, McGrath & Gavin, public relations agency
Bureau of Engraving, client

Capabilities brochure photo.

2
Christopher Caffee, Photo Synthesis, Inc., photographer
Cliff Rowe/Diane Rowe, art directors
Dennis Moran, designer
Dennis Moran Design, design firm
P.J. Dick Inc./Trumbull Corporation, clients

Impressions of construction at the Pittsburgh airport for a capabilities brochure.

3 (series)
Bob Carey, photographer
Jami Pomponi, art director
Companion Animal Association of Arizona, Inc., client

A series of photographs promoting the use of animals as companions to the elderly.

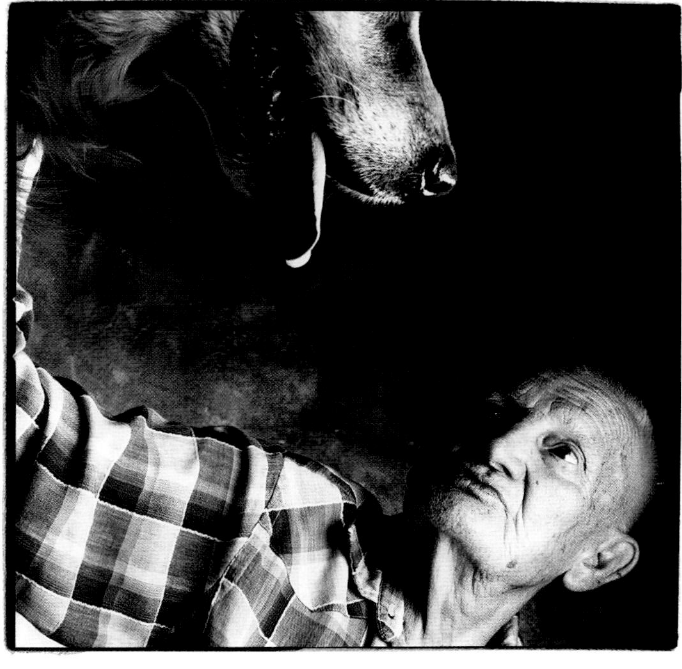

1

## Institutional

1 (series)
Abhijit Varde, photographer/art director
Ken Light, picture editor
Campaign for Human Rights, client

Fund-raising slide presentation showing children, education, caste system and landless peasantry in rural areas of the state of Maharashtra, India.

1

2

## Institutional

1 (series)
Gary Nolton, photographer
Janice Gega, designer
Nike Design, design
Nike, client

Basketball brochure.

2
Kathryn Kleinman, photographer
Jennifer Morla, art director
Jennifer Morla/Sharrie Brooks, designers
Sara Slavin, stylist
Morla Design, design firm
American President Lines, client

Corporate calendar page.

3
Ralph Daniel, photographer
Jerome Smith, art director
J. Walter Thompson, ad agency
Captain Mark Everson, United States Marine Corps, client

Brochure photograph.

3

## Institutional

1 (series)
Joanne Dugan, photographer
Michael Bierut, designer
Pentagram Design, design firm
Historic Hudson Valley, client

Annual report showing historic homes. Pictured are Washington Irving House (Sunnyside) and two views of Montgomery Place.

2
Stewart Charles Cohen, photographer
Bob Johnson, art director
Club Corporation of America, client

Brochure.

1

2

1

2

3

# Institutional

1 (series)
Marc Norberg, photographer
Frank James, designer
Nancekivell Design, design firm
The St. Paul Companies, client

Annual report.

2
Chris Hamilton, photographer
Suzy Miller, designer
Copeland Hirthler Design & Communication, design firm
Atlanta Paralympic Organizing Committee, client

Marketing brochure for "The Glory of the Games," the 1996 Atlanta Paralympic Games.

3
Nadav Kander, photographer
John Doyle, art director
Doyle Advertising & Design Group, ad agency
Amnesty International, client

Portrait of Fatima Ibrahim, a writer, speaker and union leader for Sudanese women's rights.

1

2

3

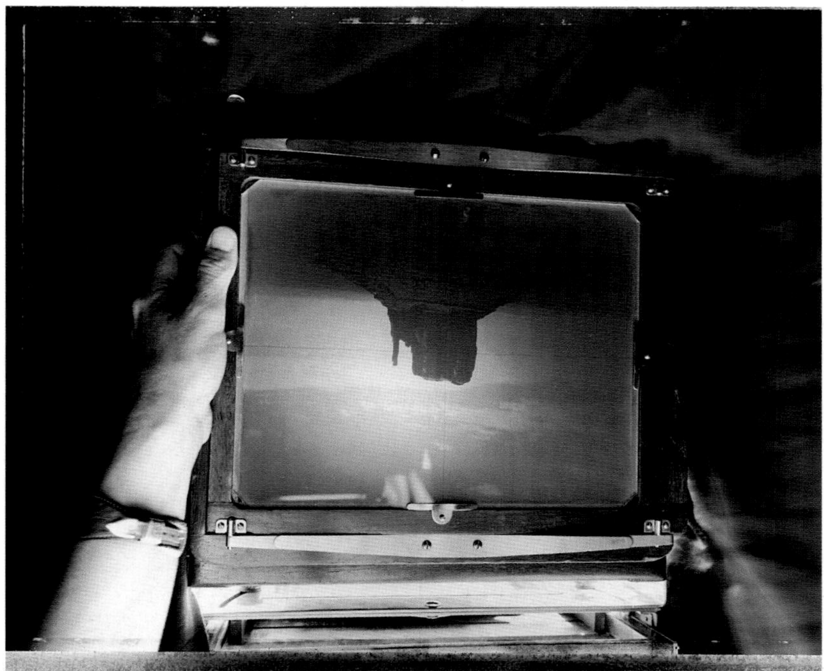

## INSTITUTIONAL

1
Terry Husebye, photographer
Steve Powell, art director
Smart Creative Services, ad agency
Pacific Bell, client

Kern County fair midway in Bakersfield, California, for PacBell Yellow Pages cover.

2
Russ Schleipman, photographer
Don Ferber, art director/designer
Ferber Design, design firm
Raytheon, client

Photograph, for an annual report, to suggest the use of avionics and missles by the military.

3 (series)
Mark Klett, Swanstock, photographer
Mary Johnson/Nancy Solomon, designers
Amon Carter Museum, curator

"Revealing Territory," photographs of the Southwest.

"Entering a Narrow Cave," used as the cover for the exhibition catalog at the Museum of Contemporary Photography, Columbia College, Chicago.

"Under the Dark Cloth," used as the cover for the exhibition catalog at the Center for Creative Photography, Tucson, Arizona.

## INSTITUTIONAL

1
Thomas Heinser, photographer
Madeleine Corson, art director
Madeleine Corson Design, design firm
Jantz Design, client

Catalog cover for "The Natural Bedroom."

2
Ian Lawrence, photographer
Randolph & Tate Associates, art consultants
Haines, Lundberg & Waehler, architects
Federal Reserve Bank of New York, client

Mural produced using the Cinescan technique.

3 (series)
David X. Tejada, photographer
Mark Mock, art director
Tim Kridle, designer
Mark Mock Design Associates, design firm
Consolidated Nevada Goldfields Corp., client

Annual report.

1

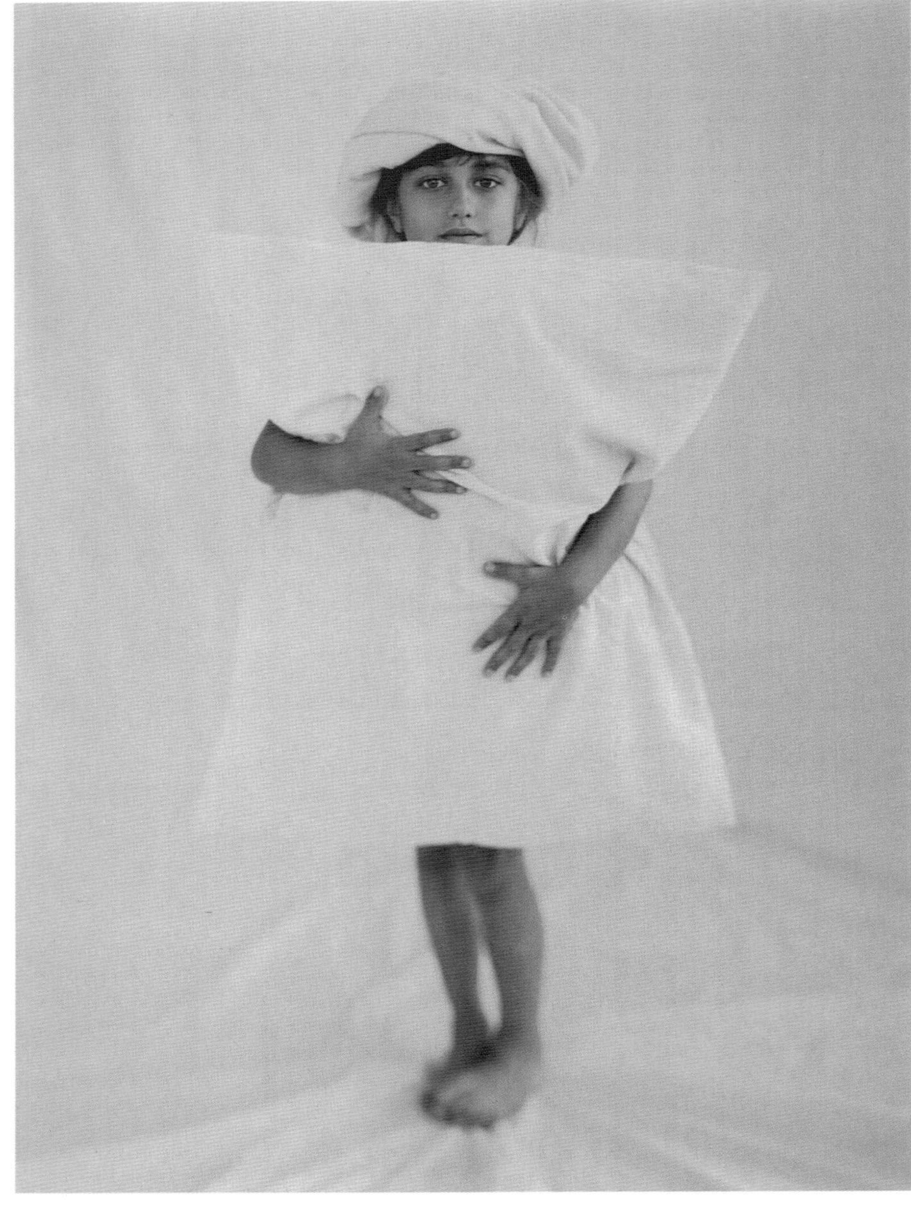

2

3

1

## Institutional

1 (series)
Gary Faye, photographer
Lana Rigsby, art director/designer
Rigsby Design, Inc., design firm
The Earth Technology Corporation, client

Photo essay in a capabilities brochure.

## INSTITUTIONAL

1 (series)
Peter Gregoire, photographer
Sandra Ray, art director/designer
Dow Jones Marketing Services, design
Dow Jones, client

Photo illustrations for a market survey of aviation managers and chief pilots.

## SELF-PROMOTION

2
Dennis Miller, photographer/designer/client

Mailer.

1

1
Allison Leach, photographer
Paul Kwong, art director
Hill/A Marketing Design Group, design firm
Southwest Texas State University/Creative Summit '92, clients

Poster. Photographer's brief was to interpret a birthday suit. Vernon Sherman, Insurance Salesman, Wharton, Texas, wore his best suit being reborn. Regrets it. Should have worn his drip-dry.

2
Joe Michl, Parallel Productions, photographer/art director/client

Studio promotion piece.

3
Jay Maisel, photographer/art director
Dave Delmonico, designer
Ice Communications, ad agency
Kodak, client

Poster. Eastman Kodak presents "Jay Maisel: Light, Gesture and Color."

4
Ralph Daniel, photographer
Ed Young, designer
Young & Martin Design, design firm
Ralph Daniel Photography, Inc., client

Poster.

1

2

3

4

1

2

## SELF-PROMOTION

1 (series)
Paul Sinkler, photographer/art director/
client

Direct mail.

2
Jim Erickson, photographer/art director
Erickson Productions, client

Source book ad.

3
Pete Turner, photographer/art director

Source book ad.

3

## Self-Promotion

1
Robb Kendrick, photographer/art director/client

Mailer.

2
Patrick Harbron, photographer/art director

Christmas card.

3 (series)
Peter Eckert, photographer/art director

Mailers.

1

2

3

1 

2

## SELF-PROMOTION

1 (series)
Gill Alkin, photographer/art director
David Shelly, designer
Gill Alkin Photography, client

2
Don Glentzer, photographer
Jay Loucks/Don Glentzer, art directors
Jay Loucks, designer
Loucks Atelier, design firm
Glentzer Photography, client

Poster announcing "The Missions," a photography exhibit at Galeria Las Vigas in El Paso, Texas.

3
Jim Scherer, photographer
Miyo Ohshima Slater, art director
Gunn Associates, design firm
Kanzaki Paper, client

Photograph from a brochure to show the printing capabilities of Preeminence gloss cover 95 lb.

3

## UNPUBLISHED

1 (series)
Flip Chalfant, photographer

© 1993 Flip Chalfant

2
David Shafer, photographer

© 1993 David Shafer

1

2

1

## Unpublished

1 (series)
Andrew Garn, photographer

Self-assigned series of architectural studies printed on gold-toned paper.

© 1993 Andrew Garn

## UNPUBLISHED

1 (series)
Melanie Eve Barocas, photographer
Ron Anderson, art director

Never used stills, commissioned by the November Group to re-elect President Bush.

© 1993 Melanie Eve Barocas

2
Joe Baraban, photographer
Bill Kauker, art director

Microsoft performance photograph.

© 1993 Joe Baraban

1

2

1

2

## Unpublished

1 (series)
Kent Barker, photographer

Fine art images from a two-month sabbatical on the Swedish island of Marstrand.

2
Peter Eckert, photographer

© 1993 Peter Eckert

3
Cheryl Klauss, photographer

© 1993 Cheryl Klauss

3

1

## Unpublished

1 (series)
William Mercer McLeod, photographer

Photographs of the photographer's daughter, Ava Ray.

© 1993 William Mercer McLeod

1

## Unpublished

1 (series)
Dave Stoecklein, photographer/art director
Stoecklein Publishing, client

Photographs for a future book.

© 1993 Dave Stoecklein

2
Clem Spalding, photographer/art director

© 1993 Clem Spalding

2

1

2

3

## Unpublished

1
Jeffrey Aaronson, photographer

© 1993 Jeffrey Aaronson

2
William Thompson, photographer

© 1993 William Thompson

3 (series)
Cristiana Ceppas, photographer

© 1993 Cristiana Ceppas

## Unpublished

1
Nicola Kountoupes, photographer

© 1993 Nicola Kountoupes

2
James Dickens, photographer

© 1993 James Dickens

3
Daniel DeSouza, photographer

© 1993 Daniel DeSouza

1

2

3

## Unpublished

1
Ron Baxter Smith, photographer
Todd Richards, art director

© 1993 Ron Baxter Smith

2
Ron Lowery, photographer/art director
Gerhard Borchers, assistant art director

© 1993 Ron Lowery

3
Karen I. Hirsch, photographer/art director

Photographer Arnold Newman.

© 1993 Karen I. Hirsch

4
Bill Geddes, photographer/art director

© 1993 Bill Geddes

1

2

3

4

## Unpublished

1
Michael O'Brien, photographer
Rick McQuiston, art director

One from a series of photographs shot for a Wieden & Kennedy Oregon Tourism campaign, never used.

© 1993 Michael O'Brien

2 (series)
Bryan Mar, photographer/art director

© 1993 Bryan Mar

1

2

Life
seems
to speed
ed on by.
Things happen in su
n such fast motion that we
at we often only see things
y see things as a whole.
a whole.
Rarely does one full
fully recognize the pletho
plethora of activity happeni
ity happening simultaneously
simultaneously

1

2

UNPUBLISHED

1
Stuart N. Dee, photographer/art director

© 1993 Stuart N. Dee

2 (series)
Daniel Peebles, Swanstock, photographer

© 1993 Daniel Peebles, Swanstock

## Unpublished

1
Harry Giglio, photographer/art director

© 1993 Harry Giglio

2
Robb Kendrick, photographer
Kathy Moran, picture editor

Mt. Everest in the Himalayan mountain range for *National Geographic*. Tom Kennedy, director of photography; Bill Graves, editor.

© 1993 Robb Kendrick

3
Glen Wexler, photographer

Jazz pianist Herbie Hancock.

© 1993 Glen Wexler

1

2

3

## Unpublished

1
Michael Schneps, photographer
Adrianne Hurndell, art director

Future book on cross dressers.

© 1993 Michael Schneps

2
Stephen Kennedy, photographer

Entrance gate to the Breese, Illinois, Avon Drive-in.

© 1993 Stephen Kennedy

3 (series)
Allan Hunter Shoemake, photographer
Jim Redzinak, designer

Work in progress on a portrait book of Special Olympics athletes. Red Flannel Design Group, design firm; Chubb & Son Inc., client.

© 1993 Allan Hunter Shoemake

1

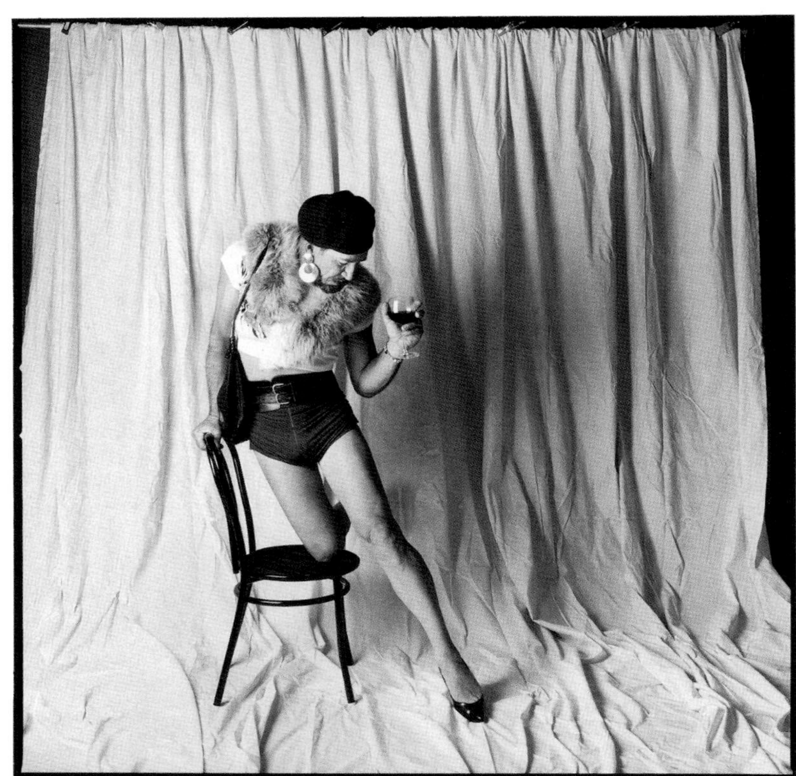

2

3

1

## Unpublished

1
Bob Stevens, photographer/art director
Robert Stevens Productions, client

© 1993 Bob Stevens

2
Alan Ross, photographer/art director

© 1993 Alan Ross

2

PART TWO

# 34

# ILLUSTRATION ANNUAL

# C A T E G O R I E S

# THE JURY

WES BAUSMITH

is the senior art director for features at *The Detroit News*. He has worked for daily newspapers, including the *Palm Beach Post* and the *Providence Journal-Bulletin* (where he designed the Sunday magazine), in an editing/design capacity for the past nine years. Bausmith is a graduate of Indiana University, where he majored in journalism and fine arts. He also attended the Art Academy of Cincinnati and concentrated on drawing and painting. Wes has had work chosen for the CA Illustration Annuals, *Print* regional annuals, the Society of Illustrators and won commendations from the Society of Newspaper Designers.

ANDREA JANETOS HYETT

has been an advertising agency art director at Foote, Cone & Belding in San Francisco for seven years. She works primarily on the Levi's account, having produced TV campaigns for 501s and Menswear and print campaigns for Youthwear and Dockers. Before joining FCB, Andrea worked as an art director and graphic designer at Mangino, Murray & Johns and Humpal, Leftwich & Sinn.

GARY KOEPKE

has been designing magazines for nearly ten years, addressing diversified audiences, from software to entertainment and fashion. He started his own business in 1987, after art directing *Musician* magazine for four years. Magnolia, Massachusetts-based Koepke has designed a wide range of publications, including *Global*, for Bull H.N. Information Systems; *26*, for Agfa Corporation; *Spin*; *Creem*; *Colors* for Benetton; and *Vibe*, a new music publication for Quincy Jones through Time Ventures.

JACKIE MERRI MEYER

is vice president/creative director of New York-based Warner Books, a Time Warner Company, and oversees 300 book jackets and cover designs per year. She has also held positions at Macmillan, McGraw-Hill, Vogue Promotion and Abraham & Strauss. Jackie is a member of the AIGA, the Art Director's Club and the Society of Illustrators where she served on the board of directors for several years. She has a BFA from Cooper Union; has taught Communication in the Design/Undergraduate Program at Parson School of Design and has lectured at the Society of Illustrators and the American Illustration Graphic Arts Weekend.

DOUG WOLFE

is president of Hawthorne/Wolfe, a design consulting firm in St. Louis. He began his career in Lancaster, Pennsylvania and in 1977 accepted a position with Regn/Califano, a corporate design office in New York. In 1982, he formed Hawthorne/Wolfe with his wife, Marta Hawthorne. The firm's work in employee publications, annual reports and marketing communications has been recognized by numerous organizations and publications. Doug was the founding president of the St. Louis chapter of the AIGA and presently serves on the AIGA's national board of directors.

## Advertising

1
Craig Frazier, illustrator/art director/designer
Frazier Design, design firm
Mill Valley Film Festival, client

Poster. $24^{1}/_{4}$ x $33^{3}/_{8}$; cut paper.

2
Brian Barrington, illustrator/art director/designer/design firm
Plain Rap Productions, client

CD cover and insert for "Pieces of the Frame." 18 x $5^{3}/_{4}$; scratchboard, acrylic and oil.

3
Bryan Leister, illustrator
Chris Noel, art director/designer
Chris Noel Design, design firm
On-Line Computer Systems, Inc., client

Packaging wrap-around. 30 x 20; oils.

4
Steve Johnson/Lou Fancher, illustrators
Michael Yuen, art director
Grey Entertainment & Media, client

Poster for a Broadway play, *Face Value*, a comedy about actors, racial stereotypes and the confusion created by taking others at face value. 14 x 21; acrylic on paper.

5
Marc Mongeau, illustrator/designer
Louise Fugere/Maryse Pelletier, art directors
Jean R. Beauchesne, design firm
Théâtre Populaire du Québec, client

Poster. 16 x 21; watercolor.

1

2

3

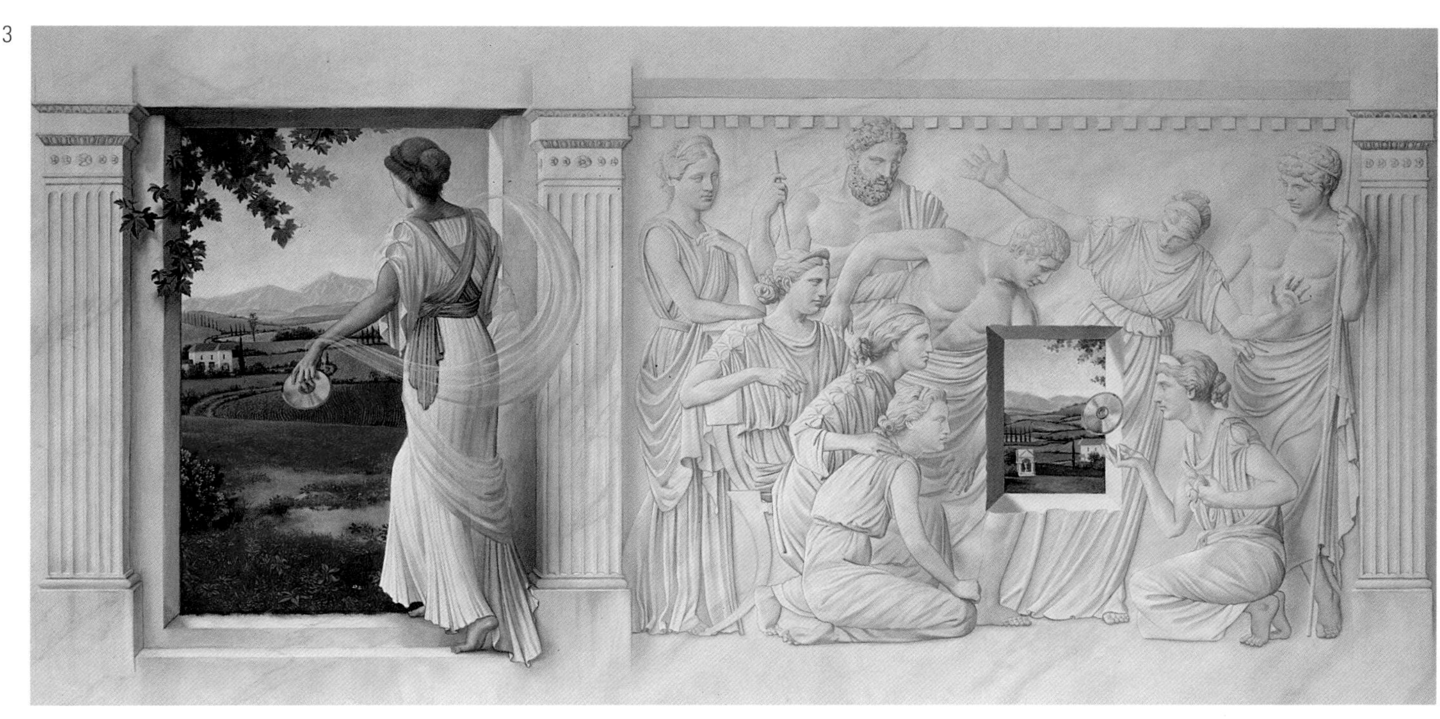

4

5

1

## ADVERTISING

1 (series)
Jerry LoFaro, illustrator
Scott Willy, art director
Kirk Nugent, designer
Cranfill Advertising Agency, ad agency
GTE North Classic, client

Giants of Golf promotion posters for the senior PGA golf tour: Ray Floyd, Chi Chi Rodriguez and Arnold Palmer. 13 x 20; acrylic, airbrush and painted.

## Advertising

1
Melinda Beck, illustrator
Polygram Records, design firm/client

CD cover. 9 x 9; scratchboard.

2
Hayes Henderson, illustrator
Roger Gorman, art director/designer
Reiner Design, design firm
Ray Lynch/Windham Hill Records, clients

CD cover "The Sky of Mind." 12 x 12; oil.

3
Mike Benny, illustrator
Bob Beyn, art director
Vicki Rand, designer
Seraphein Beyn, ad agency
Shanley's Bar & Grill, client

Shanley's Irish Music Festival & 13th Anniversary Celebration poster. 16 x 18; acrylic.

1

2

3

## ADVERTISING

1 (series)
Marvin Mattelson, illustrator
June Robinson/Susan Armstrong, art directors
McCaffrey & McCall, ad agency
Arts & Entertainment Cable Network, client

Bus posters, headline: Changing the Face of Television. 12 x 12; oil on ragboard.

2
Stasys Eidrigevicius, illustrator
James Seacat, art director
Actors Theatre of Louisville, client

Poster. 18 x 24; pastel.

3
Paul Davis, illustrator/designer
Frances Myers, art director
Eric Baker, designer
The Body Shop, client

Poster for Blue Corn. 12 x 18; acrylic on board.

4
Gregory Bridges, illustrator/art director
Gregory Bridges/Jenni Vella, designers
Inhaus Design, design firm
Australasian Memory, client

Ad for distributors of third party memory boards, headline: No Problem. 16 x 12¼; gouache on board.

1

2

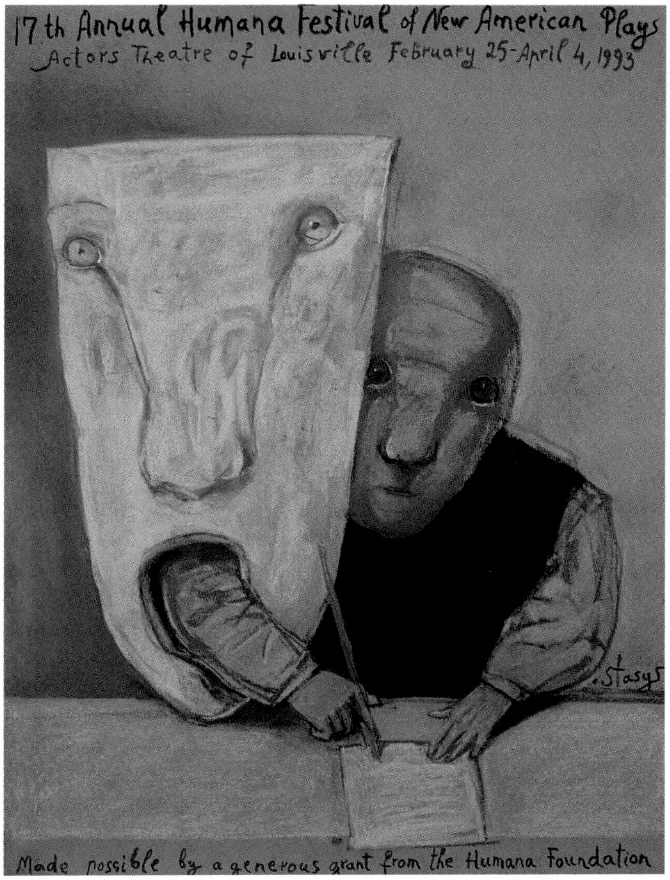
17th Annual Humana Festival of New American Plays
Actors Theatre of Louisville February 25-April 4, 1993
Stasys
Made possible by a generous grant from the Humana Foundation

3

BLUE CORN
Paul Davis

4

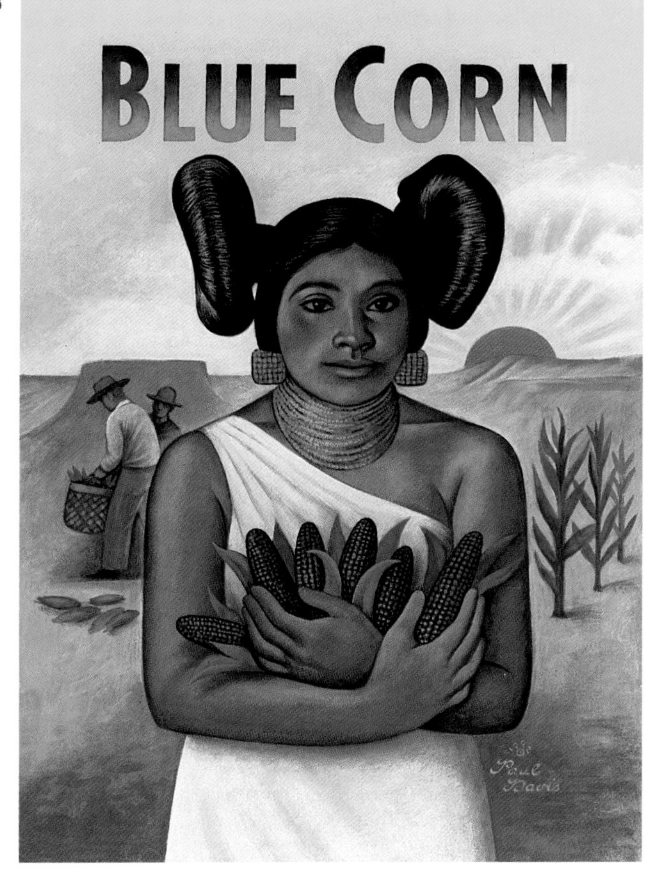

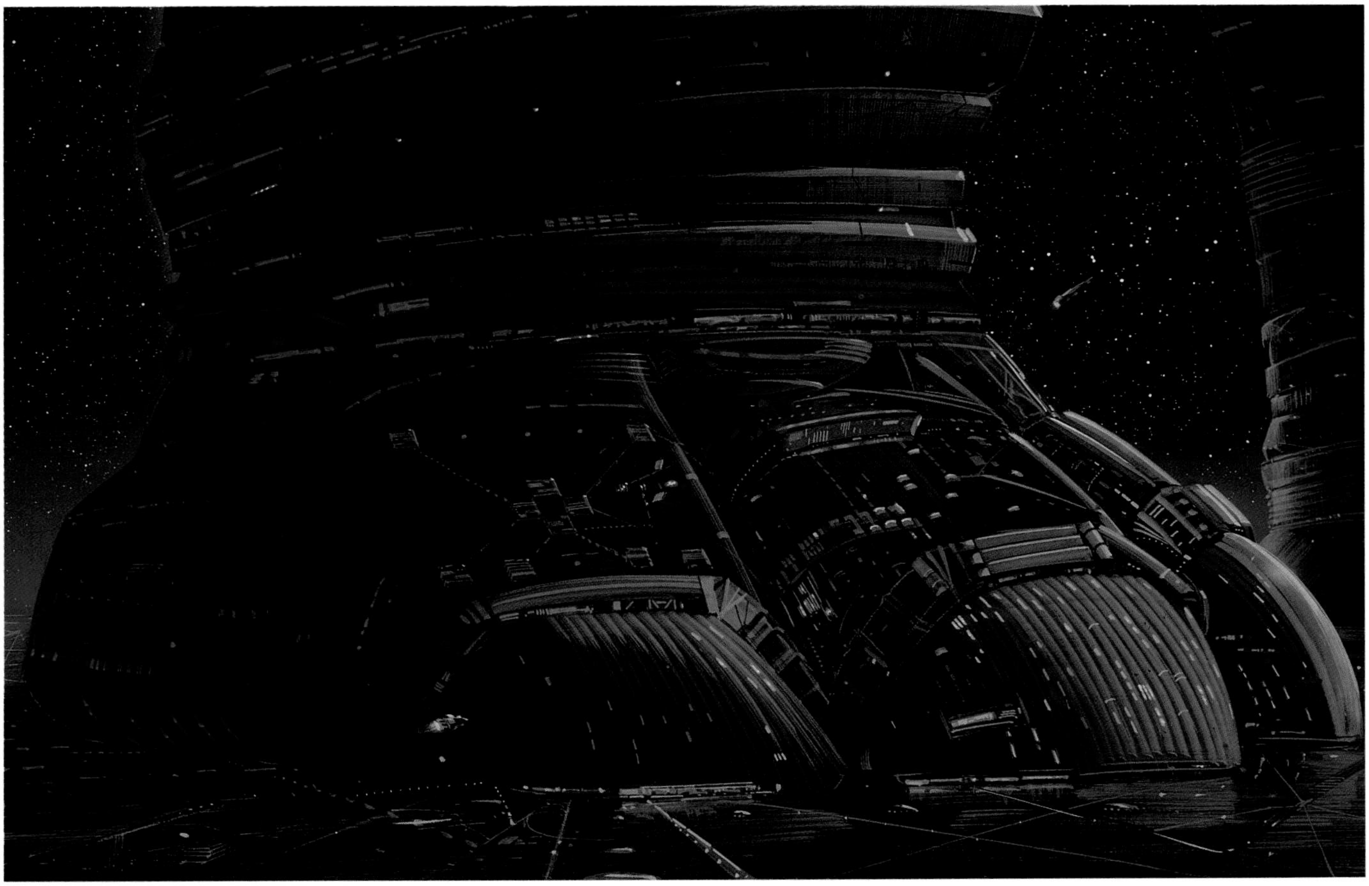

1

2

## ADVERTISING

1
Joel Nakamura, illustrator
Andy Baltimore, art director
Sony Mediana, design
Don Grusin/GRP Records, clients

CD cover. 24 x 24; mixed media.

2
Albert Rocarols, illustrator
Robert Gonzalez, art director
Gramm Werbeagentur, ad agency
Henkell & Söhnle, client

Ad and poster to introduce Spanish Cava Codorniu in Germany, headline: Time for a New Bubbling. Acrylic on canvas.

3
James McMullan, illustrator
Richard Clewes, art director/designer
Clewes & Company, ad agency
Brains II, client

Poster for Canadian Used Computers Ltd., Canadian Systems Maintenance, headline: Gone Thinking. 9 x 5; watercolor.

3

## ADVERTISING

1 (series)
Michael Bartalos, illustrator
Masaaki Hiromura, art director/designer
Hiromura Design Office, design firm
Ryohin Keikaku Co. Ltd., client

Department store monthly promotional postcards. Various sizes; linoleum block print.

2
Brad Holland, illustrator
Claudia Brambilla, art director/designer
J. Walter Thompson Italia, ad agency
Ansaldo, client

Ad headline: Without moving an inch, we see the sun rise 70 times a day. 16 x 20; acrylic.

1

2

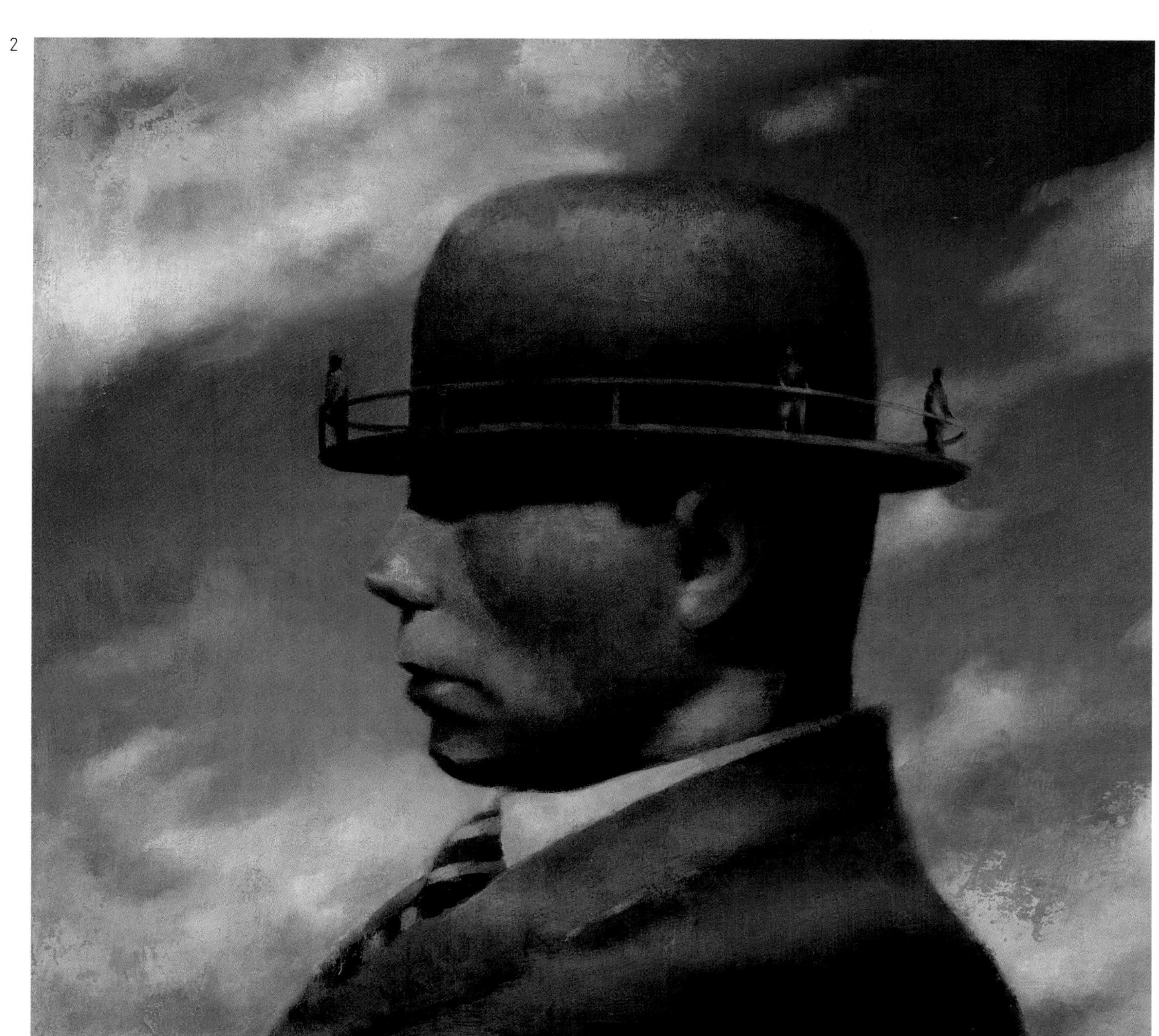

1

2

## Advertising

1
Mark A. Fredrickson, illustrator
Steve Reaves, art director/designer
Intralink Film & Design, design
Warner Bros., client

*Dennis the Menace* standee for theater display.
30 x 40; acrylic.

2 (series)
David Kacmarynski, illustrator/art director
Ann Perrizo, art director/designer
Studio Graphics, design firm
Door Peninsula Winery, client

Wine labels. 6 x 5¾; oil.

1

2

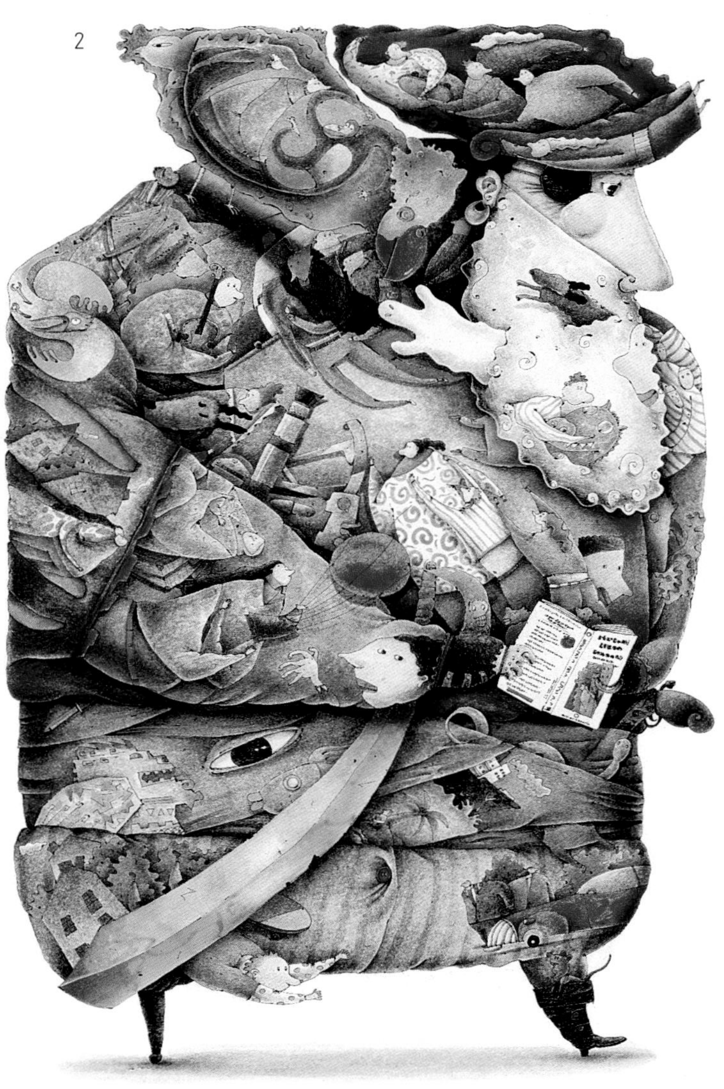

3

## ADVERTISING

1
Tom Curry, illustrator
Pat Flanagan, art director/designer
Russek Advertising, ad agency
New York City Opera, client

Poster for *The Student Prince*. 12 x 19; acrylic on hardboard.

2
Marc Mongeau, illustrator
Chantale Girard, art director
Québec/Amérique, publisher/client

Poster for a collection of stories for young readers. 11 x 19; watercolor.

3
Peter D'Angelo, illustrator
Sara Rotman, art director
Columbia/Ruff House, client

CD cover for "Tricks of the Shade." $5^{1}/_{4}$ x $5^{1}/_{2}$; colored pencil and gouache on wood.

## ADVERTISING

1
James Yang, illustrator
Bob Defrin, art director
Jody Rovin, designer
Atlantic Records, design
East West Records/Atlantic Records, clients

Happyhead CD cover "Give Happyhead." 7 1/4 x 13 3/4; acrylic.

2 (series)
Laura Levine, illustrator
Alli Truch, art director
Verve/Polygram Records, client

CD covers for Essential Series. 18 x 18; acrylic on Masonite.

1

2

BILLIE HOLIDAY
"LADY DAY"
SONGS OF LOST LOVE
L.L.

ELLA FITZGERALD
THE GREAT SONGS
L.L.

SARAH VAUGHAN
"SASSY"
THE GREAT SONGS
L.L.

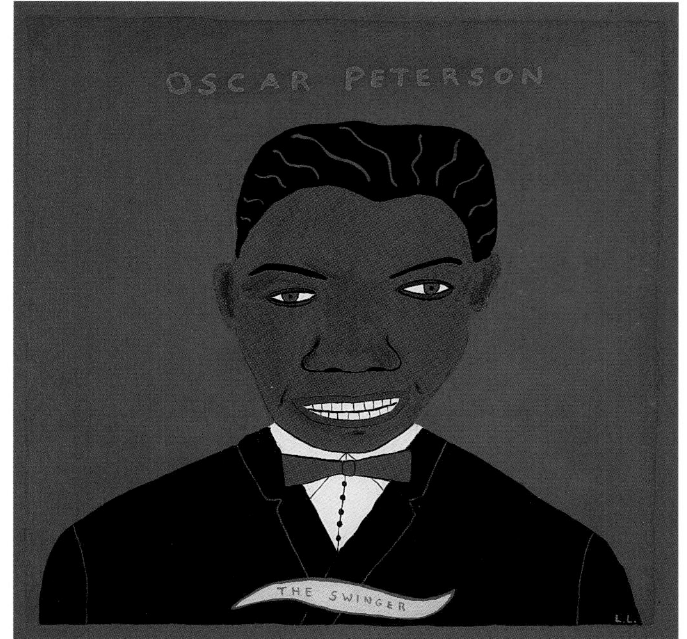
OSCAR PETERSON
THE SWINGER
L.L.

ADVERTISING

1
Scott Menchin, illustrator
Scott Wadler, art director
Laurie Hinzman, designer
Comedy Central/MTV Network, client

T-shirt art, "Free Comedy." 8 x 10; ink.

2
Barbara Nessim, illustrator
Keith Potter, art director
Foote, Cone & Belding, ad agency
Levi Strauss & Co., client

"Seated Figure #2" for Levi's 550 Relaxed Fit Jeans ad. 9 x 11 1/2; ink on paper.

3
Richard Wehrman, illustrator
Mike Hogan, art director/designer
Wolf Winterkorn Lillis, ad agency
Precision Filters, Inc., client

Electronic signal conditioners ad. 12 x 10 1/2; acrylic on board.

1

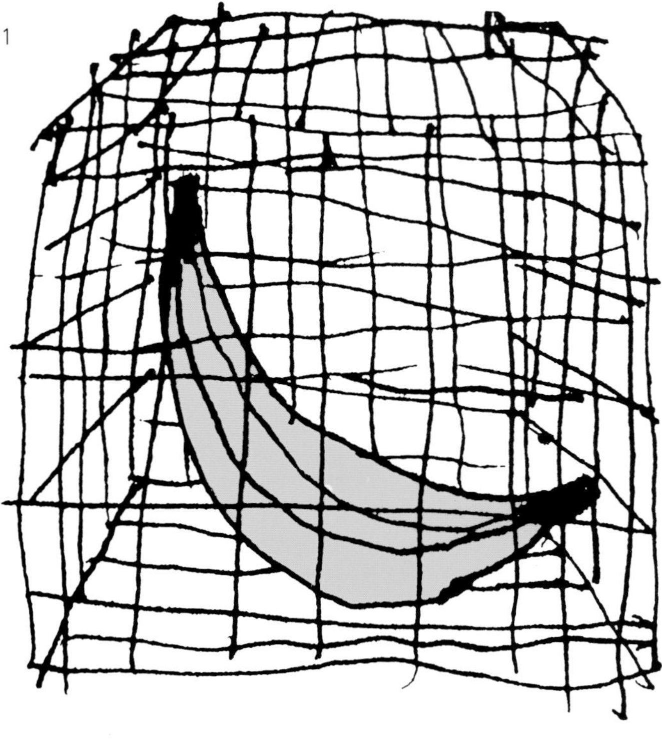


2

3

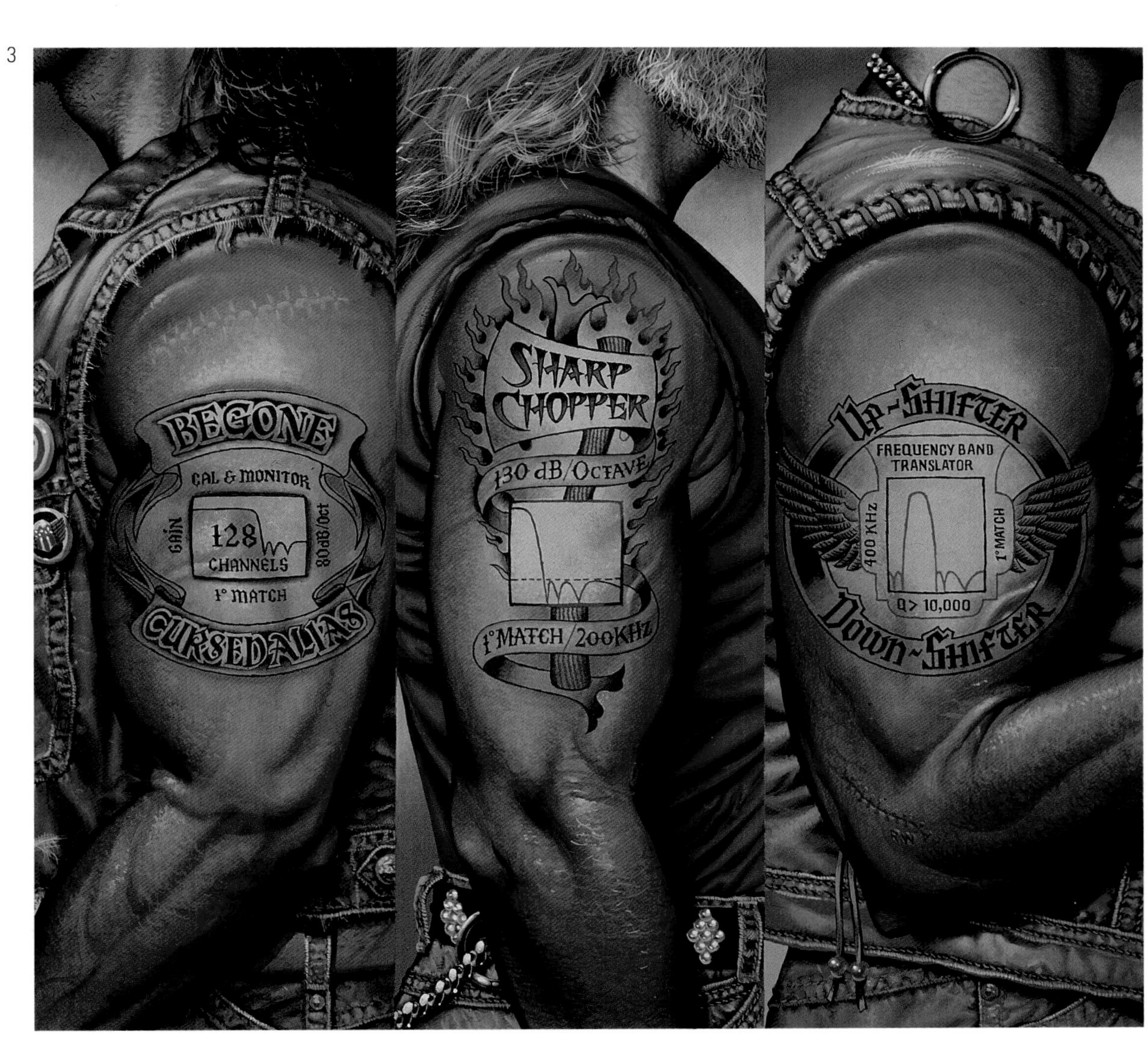
BEGONE
CAL & MONITOR
GAIN
128
CHANNELS
80dB/Oct
1° MATCH
CURSED ALIAS
SHARP CHOPPER
130 dB/OCTAVE
1°MATCH/200KHz
UP-SHIFTER
FREQUENCY BAND
TRANSLATOR
400 KHz
1° MATCH
Q > 10,000
DOWN-SHIFTER

1

2

## Advertising

1 (series)
Scott McKowen, illustrator/art director/designer
The Shaw Festival, Niagara-on-the-Lake, client

Poster ad images promoting plays by George Bernard Shaw. Various sizes; scratchboard.

2
Jordin Isip, illustrator
Georgie Stout, art director
Georgie Stout/David Weeks, designers
Steady State, design firm
UI/Sasha Frere-Jones, clients

UI CD cover. $12^{1}/_{8}$ x $12^{1}/_{8}$; mixed media.

3
Corbert Gauthier, illustrator
Kevin Samuels, art director
Bozell Worldwide, Inc., ad agency
Valvoline Oil Co., client

Brochure cover showing Valvoline's environmental concern. 14 x $7^{3}/_{4}$; oil.

3

## Advertising

1
Curtis Parker, illustrator
Brad Ghormley, art director
Smit Ghormley Lofgreen, design firm
Childsplay Theater, client

Poster for *The Nightingale.* 17 x 17; acrylic on canvas.

2
Roy Carruthers, illustrator
David Bartels, art director
Brian Barclay, designer
Bartels & Company, Inc., ad agency
Electronic Data Systems, client

EDS assists companies in integrating computers into their businesses, ad headline: Quite often the secret to success is knowing which strings to pull. 20 x 13; oil.

3
James McMullan, illustrator
Michael di Capua, art director
Angela Gier, designer
Michael di Capua Books/Harper Collins, clients

Children's book poster. 6 x 9; watercolor.

1

2

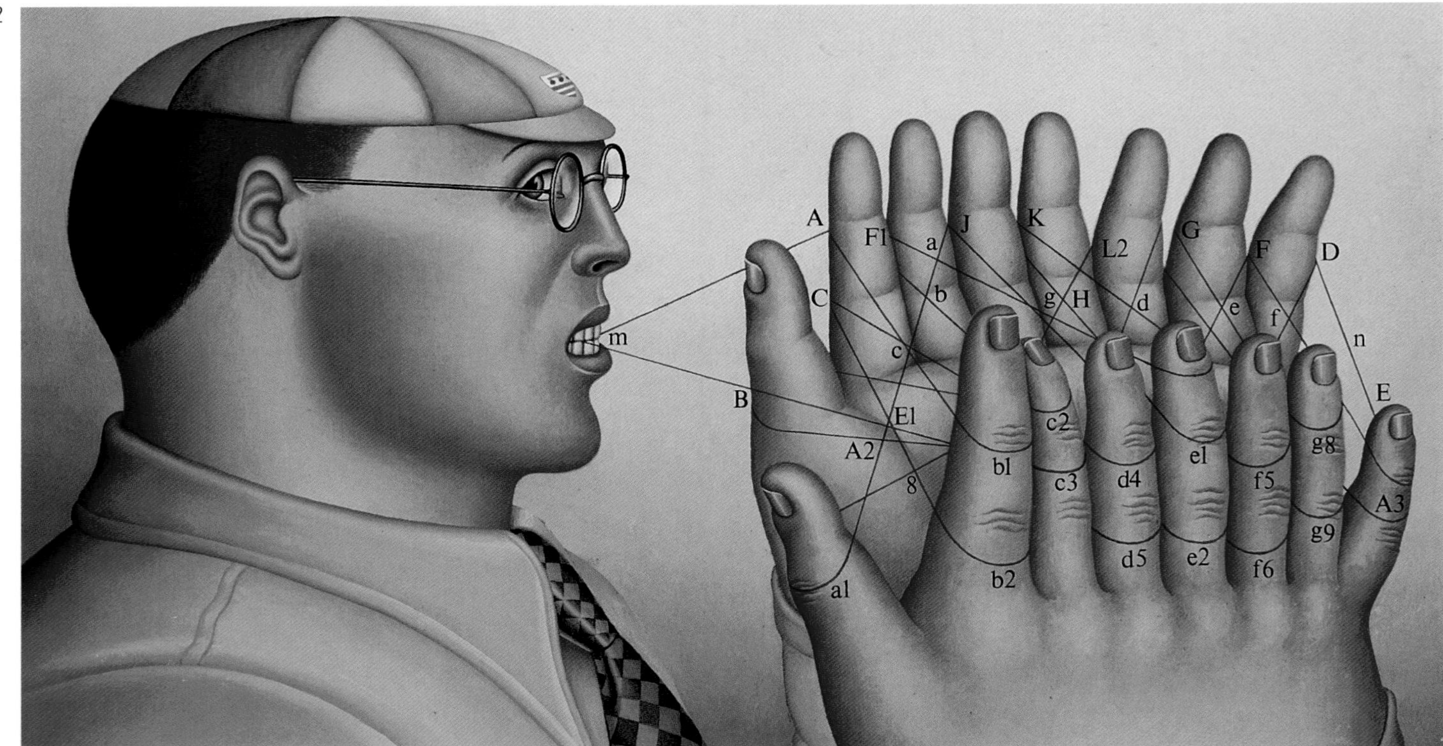

3

THE NOISY GIANTS' TEA PARTY

By KATE AND JIM McMULLAN

POLICE

MICHAEL DI CAPUA BOOKS · HARPER COLLINS

1

2

## Books

1
Michael J. Deas, illustrator
Barbara Leff, art director
Ballantine Books, client

*The Vanished Child*, a novel centering on the 1887 murder of a New England millionaire and the subsequent disappearance of his grandson, the only witness. $12^{1}/_{2}$ x $19^{1}/_{2}$; oil on panel.

2 (series)
Martha Paulos, illustrator
Fly Productions, art director/designer/design firm
Chronicle Books, client

*Felines, Great Poets on Notorious Cats.* 16 x 13; linocut.

1

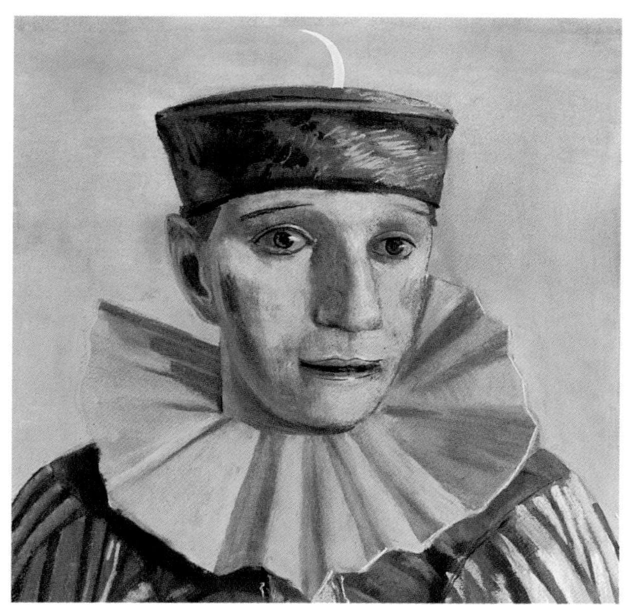

## BOOKS

1 (series)
John Collier, illustrator
Alex Jay, art director/designer
Studio J, art director/design firm
Byron Preiss, publisher
Viking/Penguin, client

*Petrouchka*, jacket and interior illustrations.
Various sizes; pastel.

## Books

1 (series)
Joe Ciardiello, illustrator/art director
Patrick JB Flynn, art director/designer
Patrick JB Flynn Design, design firm
Spanfeller Press, client

Drawings from *Like Jazz*: Chet Baker, Jimmy Rushing, Miles Davis, Rahsaan Roland Kirk and Ella Fitzgerald. Various sizes; pen and ink.

1

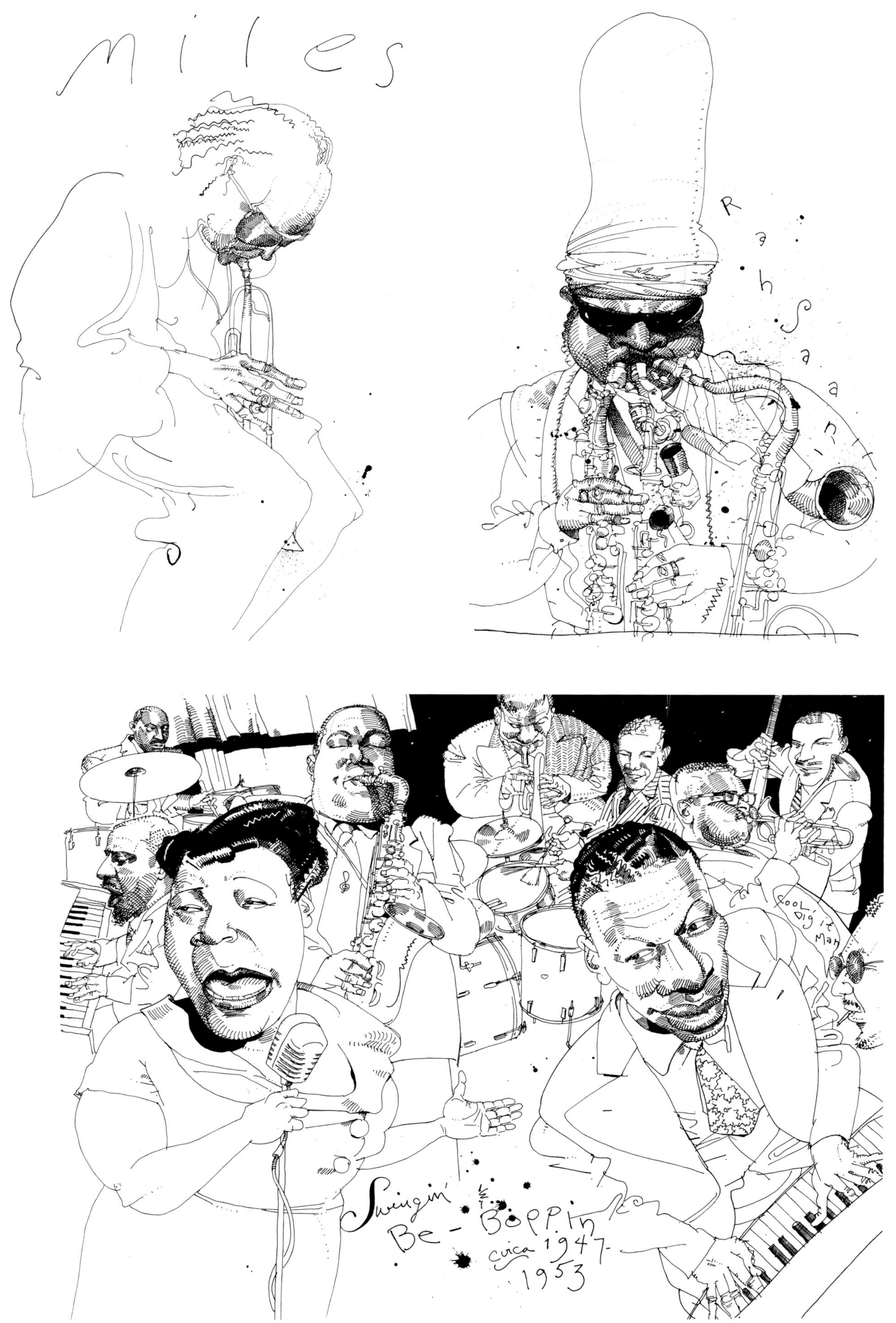
miles
Rahsaan
Cool Dig it Man
Swingin' & Be-Boppin
circa 1947-1953

1

2

3

## Books

1 (series)
Gary Kelley, illustrator
Rita Marshall, art director
Louise Fili, designer
Louise Fili Ltd., design firm
Creative Editions, client

Illustrations for *The Necklace*. Various sizes; pastel on paper.

2
Tom Curry, illustrator
Kym Abrams, art director/designer
Kym Abrams Design, design firm
Scott, Foresman & Company, client

Children's book interior illustration of *Turtle's Race With a Bear*. 10½ x 14½; acrylic on hardboard.

3
José Ortega, illustrator
Susan Mitchell, art director
Marc J. Cohen, designer
Vintage International, client

Novel about a man who runs a brothel, *Body Snatcher*. 6 x 9; pencil, copier, colored papers.

1

2

## Books

1
Michael J. Deas, illustrator
Elizabeth Parisi, art director
Scholastic, Inc., client

A novel about friendship between two young women that ultimately ends in tragedy, *The Empty Summer.* 16½ x 24½; oil on panel.

2
Thom Sevalrud, illustrator
Mary Opper, art director/designer
McGraw-Hill Ryerson, client

*Values* examines our individual values and human interaction. 9¼ x 13¾; watercolor, acrylic, Prismacolor.

3
Robert Hynes, illustrator
Robin Benjamin, art director/designer
Silver Burdett & Ginn, client

*On the Horizon*, a reading book for eight- to nine-year-olds. 18 x 12; acrylic.

3

## Books

1
Janet Atkinson, illustrator
Michael Accordino, art director
St. Martin's Press, client

Cover for *Night of the Cat*, a mystery about a young schoolteacher who becomes a policewoman to watch over the city streets. 6 x 9; acrylic.

2
Lisa Falkenstern/Milton Charles, illustrators
Milton Charles, art director/designer
Milton Charles Design, design firm
Delphinium Books, client

*Shares and Other Fictions* by Richard Stern. 12½ x 16; oil.

3 (series)
Murray Kimber, illustrator
Kelly Michele de Regt, art director
Goddard-Zaxis Publishing Inc., design firm
Eaton's, client

*Keeping a Canadian Christmas*, a collection of stories, essays, games and recipes. Various sizes; oil on canvas.

1

2

3

## Books

1 (series)
Rob Roth, illustrator
Patrice Fodero, art director
Atheneum Publishers, client

*And in the Beginning* describes how Mahtmi created the first man from the dark rich earth of Mount Kilimanjaro and gave him a gift marking him as special. 25 x 16; watercolor.

1

1

## Books

1 (series)
Wendell Minor, illustrator/designer
Anne Dieble, art director
Wendell Minor Design, design firm
Clarion Books, client

In the book *Red Fox Running*, rhyming text follows the experiences of a red fox as it searches across a wintry landscape for food. Various sizes; watercolor on cold press.

## Books

1
Cathleen Toelke, illustrator
Ruth Ross, art director
Random House, client

The novel *Wife* examines an Indian woman's struggles with social class and cultural change in adapting to life in America. 6 x 9; gouache.

2
Bill Russell, illustrator
Amy Hill, art director
Viking Penguin, client

A wife plots the murder of her husband in *Dolores Claiborne*. The illustration shows the setting for the murder. 8 x 6¾; scratchboard.

## For Sale

3
Etienne Delessert, illustrator/art director
Delessert & Marshall, design firm
Musée des Arts Décoratifs, client

Poster. 18 x 24; silkscreen.

1

2

3

## For Sale

1 (series)
Linda Montgomery, illustrator/designer
Maxine Rombout, art director
Pierre Belvedere Inc., client

Greeting cards. 30 x 40; acrylic on canvas.

1

1

2

## For Sale

1
Milton Glaser, illustrator/art director/designer
Milton Glaser, Inc., design firm
ECO Marketing & Publicity, client

T-shirt celebrating Leonardo da Vinci. 8½ x 14; pen and ink, paper collage.

2
Melinda Beck, illustrator
Patrick Flynn, art director
The Progressive Magazine, design/client

Art for a calendar using a 1971 quote from Angela Davis, "If they come for me in the morning, they will come for you at night." 11 x 11; scratchboard.

3
Illica Pozzatti, illustrator

Gallery portrait of Francesco Clemente. 18 x 24; watercolor.

3

1

## For Sale

1 (series)
Chris Hopkins, illustrator/designer
John Wiebusch, art director
Chris Hopkins Illustration, design firm
National Football League Properties, Inc., client

Football trading cards: Keith Byars, Earnest Byner, Steve Largent and Ken O'Brian. 11 x 17; oil on Masonite.

1

## For Sale

1
Julia Gran, illustrator/designer
Connie Sherman, art director
Black & White Dog Studio, design firm
How Charming Inc., client

Umbrella, "Soaked to the Gills." 8" triangle; pen and ink.

2 (series)
Martha Anne Booth, illustrator/art director/designer
First Impressions, client

Greeting cards. Various sizes; oil pastel on paper.

2

## For Sale

1
Norman Walker, illustrator/art director/designer
Santa Fean, ad agency
Carol Thorton Gallery, client

Poster. 40 x 51; oil.

2
Mark Stutzman, illustrator
Terrence McCaffrey, art director
Howard Paine, designer
United States Postal Service, client

Postage stamp honoring Elvis Presley. 6½ x 5; airbrush.

## Editorial

3
Julian Allen, illustrator
Teresa Fernandes, art director
Travel Holiday, client

"The Painted Island," a charming haven off the Breton coast.
12 x 18; watercolor.

1

2

3

## EDITORIAL

1
Doug Aitken, illustrator
Lucy Bartholomay, art director
The Boston Globe Magazine, client

"Rebels Without a Cause." Growing up in liberal Amherst in the late '60s, these high school hippies found that a basketball challenge was the only form of revolution they could shoot for. 10½ x 13; mixed media.

2
Benoit, illustrator
Lee Lorenz, art director
The New Yorker, client

Artist's Notebook, "Winter Wonderland." 11 x 14; oil.

3
Gary Baseman, illustrator
Palma McGowan, designer
M Magazine, client

Article about testosterone, "Extract of Virility." 8½ x 8½; mixed media.

4
Marie Lessard, illustrator
Jocelyne Fournel, art director
MTL, client

Montréal lifestyle magazine, "Savoring the Prickly Pear," an epiphany to eau de vie. 6 x 6⅞; linocut and dyes.

5
James Yang, illustrator
Patti Nelson, art director
The Northeast, client

Magazine article, "The Object of My Affliction," is a halfhearted tribute to love. 10 x 11; acrylic.

1

2

3

4

5

1

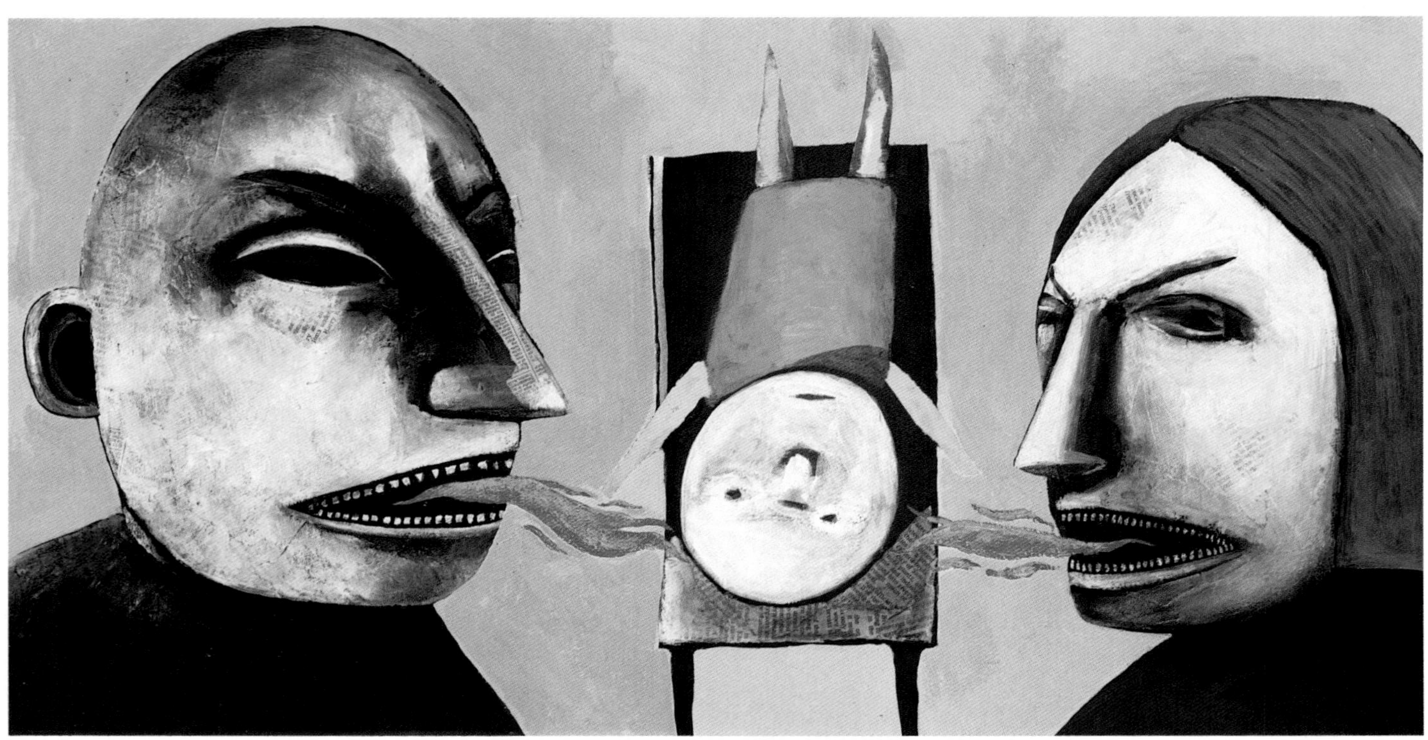

2

3

## Editorial

1 (series)
Jordin Isip, illustrator
Rob George, art director/designer
Psychology Today, client

Magazine article, "Why Kids Kill Parents." Various sizes; mixed media.

2
Jeffrey Fisher, illustrator
Tim Cook, art director
Suzuki Design, design firm
American Diabetes Association, client

Association magazine *Diabetes Forecast* article, "The Importance of Exercise." 10 x 12; mixed media and collage.

3
C.F. Payne, illustrator
D.J. Stout, art director
Texas Monthly, client

Article on Ross Perot in the White House. 12 x 16; oil, acrylic, pencil, ink and airbrush.

## Editorial

1
Michael Bartalos, illustrator
Mark Porter, art director/designer
Evening Standard Magazine, client

Painting to accompany an article concerning London cinema houses. 7 x 10; airbrush and gouache on paper.

2 (series)
John Gurche, illustrator
Allen Carroll/Nicholas Kirilloff, art directors
National Geographic, client

"Dinosaurs" article: Pachycephalosaurus battering a rival male; a nesting Saurolophus; young Edmontosaurus browse in a conifer forest with a Tyrannosaurus lurking among the trees. Various sizes; acrylic.

1

2

## Editorial

1
Lilla Rogers, illustrator
Fabian Cooperman, art director
Oracle, client

Magazine article on the Golden Rule, a mathematical formula, "Predicting the Utility of the Non Unique Index." 12 x 16; ink and cut paper.

2
Andrea Ventura, illustrator
Chris Curry, art director
The New Yorker, client

Illustration of Kurt Masur, music director of the New York Philharmonic Symphony, for the orchestra listings. 11½ x 15; charcoal and acrylic.

3
Rafal Olbinski, illustrator
Judy Garlan, art director
The Atlantic, client

Magazine article, "Problem Adoptions." 16 x 20; acrylic on canvas.

1

2

3

1

2

3

4

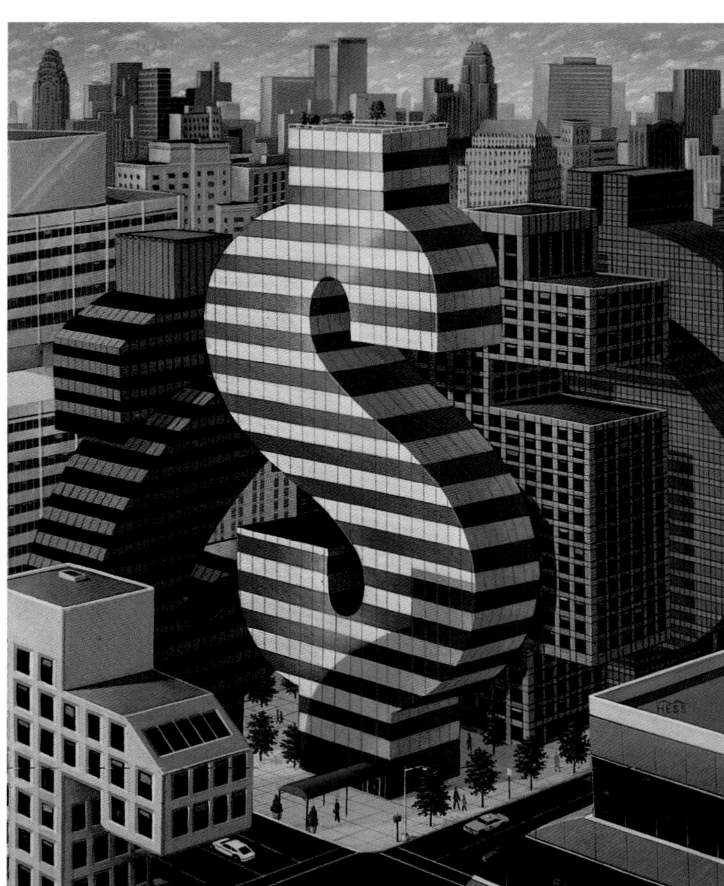


## Editorial

1
Gary Taxali, illustrator
Susan Meingast, art director
Madame au Foyer, client

Magazine article on bad manners. "La politesse, vous connaissez?" 31 x 22; alkyd on Masonite.

2
Douglas Fraser, illustrator
Steven Hoffman, art director
Sports Illustrated, client

Article on the decline of the Soviet sports empire, "Soviet Disunion." 12 x 8; alkyd on paper.

3
Charles Barnes, illustrator
Fred Woodward, art director
Fred Woodward/Gail Anderson/Debra Bishop/Cathy Gilmore-Barnes/Angela Skouras/Geraldine Hessler, designers
Rolling Stone, client

Little Richard, "I have seen people foaming at the mouth and just wanting to touch me." Portrait for the 25th anniversary issue of the magazine. 13 x 15¾; film positive, paper, acrylic.

4
Mark Hess, illustrator
Richard Hess/Alma Phipps, art directors
Chief Executive, client

14 x 19; acrylic on canvas.

1

## Editorial

1 (series)
Judith Reed, illustrator/designer
Cathy Kostreba, art director
Bon Appetit, client

Magazine article "Entrées" for a special Light & Easy edition. 7 x 9½; mat acrylic.

2
Rob Barber, illustrator
Jana Khalifa, art director
Gallery, client

Magazine section on spring break, sports and activities. 16 x 16; acrylic on canvas.

2

1

2

3

4

5

6

## Editorial

1
Hayes Henderson, illustrator
David Carson, art director/designer
Raygun, client

Magazine illustration for "99.9 F" Suzanne Vega's latest hit song. 9 x 9; oil.

2
David Beck, illustrator
Therese Shecter, art director
Chicago Tribune, client

Article questions some of Sigmund Freud's theories on psychoanalysis. 9 x 9; mixed media.

3
Douglas Fraser, illustrator
Paul Roelofs, art director
Western Living, client

Magazine article on over-protective parents, "Climate of Fear." 10 x 12; alkyd on paper.

4
Jacques Cournoyer, illustrator
Jocelyne Fournel, art director/designer
MTL, client

Montréal magazine article, "Exorcised Fear." 8 x 10; acrylic.

5
Don Asmussen, illustrator/designer
Felix Grabowski, art director
The Detroit News, client

Restaurants thrive during local theater's presentation of *Phantom of the Opera*, "Bravo & Bon Appétit." 14 x 22; pen and ink, watercolor and collage.

6
Edmund Guy, illustrator
Fred Woodward, art director
Rolling Stone, client

Record column review of "Neneh's Hot Homebrew." $9\frac{1}{4}$ x $12\frac{1}{2}$.

1

CHURCH
lets go eat
To the lord let
praises be
It's time for dinner
Now let's go eat
lets eat
Lyle Lovett

2

Paul Davis © 1992

3

TEMPLES OF AMERICAN FLY~FISHING
YELLOWSTONE WATERS
CATSKILL WATERS
BROWN TROUT
Salmo trutta
YELLOWSTONE CUTTHROAT
Oncorhynchus bouvieri
BROOK TROUT
Salvelinus fontinalis
RAINBOW TROUT
Oncorhynchus mykiss

4 

5 

## EDITORIAL

1
Joel Nakamura, illustrator
Brad Stone, art director/designer
Music Express, design
The Wherehouse, client

In-store magazine featuring an illustration of the Lyle Lovett song "Church," from Joshua Judges Ruth's album. 14 x 18; mixed media.

2
Paul Davis, illustrator
Fred Woodward, art director
Fred Woodward/Gail Anderson/Debra Bishop/Cathy Gilmore-Barnes/ Angela Skouras/Geraldine Hessler, designers
Rolling Stone, client

Madonna, "When I was growing up, I wanted to be a nun...I saw nuns as superstars." Portrait for the 25th anniversary issue of the magazine. 12 x 15; acrylic on wood.

3
Dugald Stermer, illustrator/designer
Matthew Drace, art director
Men's Journal, client

Article on fly-fishing. 20 x 12; pencil and watercolor on Arches paper.

4
Robert M. Pastrana, illustrator
Nancy Duckworth, art director
Los Angeles Times Magazine, client

Article about jazz in Los Angeles, "Jazz Blues." 8¼ x 10¼; watercolor.

5
Philippe Weisbecker, illustrator
Jane Palecek, art director
Health, client

Magazine feature, "When Your Office Calls in Sick." 7½ x 9½; ink and watercolor.

## EDITORIAL

1
Alan E. Cober, illustrator
Fred Woodward, art director
Fred Woodward/Gail Anderson/Debra Bishop/Cathy Gilmore-Barnes/Angela Skouras/Geraldine Hessler, designers
Rolling Stone, client

Ice-T. Portrait for the 25th anniversary issue of the magazine. 9 x 12; ink and watercolor.

2
Janet Woolley, illustrator
Carol Layton, designer/art director
Worth, client

Magazine feature, "Waiting for the Dough." 18 x 22; acrylic, photo montage.

3 (series)
José Ortega, illustrator
Ronda Rubenstein, art director
Amid Capeci, designer
Esquire, client

Magazine article about lying in the workplace, "100% Pure Honest." 3 x 3; scratchboard, watercolor, wax crayon.

4
Brad Holland, illustrator
Kerig Pope/Tom Staebler, art directors
Playboy, client

Magazine article, "Malcolm X Remembered" by Alex Haley. As rappers, historians and Spike Lee lay claim to the martyred black leader, his late friend and biographer recalls the man. 14 x 14; acrylic on panel.

1

2

3

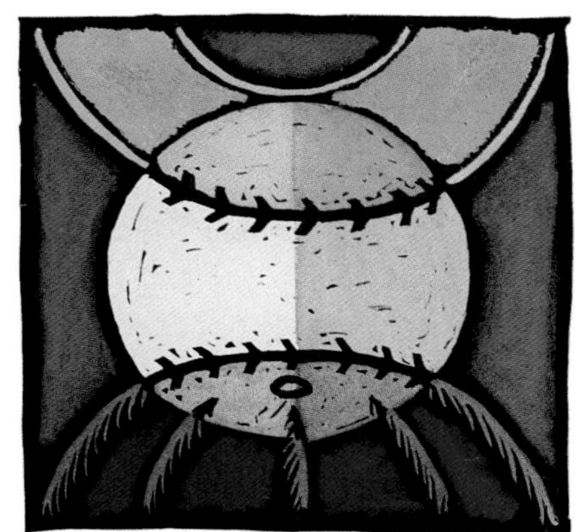

4

1

2

## EDITORIAL

1
Gary Kelley, illustrator
John Korpics, art director/designer
Premiere, client

Serialized fiction about Hollywood behind-the-scenes, "The Blue Screen." 16 x 20; pastel on paper.

2
Jacques Cournoyer, illustrator
Jocelyne Fournel, art director/designer
MTL, client

Montréal magazine article on the involvement of the church in contemporary issues, "Let's Get Involved." 12 x 12; acrylic.

3
Rick Sealock, illustrator
Claire Innes, art director/designer
Detroit Free Press, client

Article about a women-only ranch where they bond while doing chores and herding cows. 12½ x 8½; watercolor, acrylic, pastel, collage.

3

## EDITORIAL

1
Mirko Ilić, illustrator
Steven Heller, art director/designer
The New York Times Book Review, client

Review of *Preparing for the Twenty-first Century.*
8 x 12; scratchboard.

2
Jody Hewgill, illustrator
Georges Haroutiun, art director
M.A.G. Graphics, design firm
The University of Western Ontario, client

Alumni magazine article on narcolepsy, "Day Dreamers."
11 x 10¼; acrylic.

3
C.F. Payne, illustrator
Robert Priest, art director
Gentlemen's Quarterly, client

Clinton and Gore offer a busted country one last deal, "Goin' South." 16 x 18; oil, acrylic, ink, pencil, watercolor, airbrush.

1

2

3

## Editorial

1
Richard Downs, illustrator
Nancy Duckworth, art director
Steven Banks, designer
Los Angeles Times Magazine, client

"Burnout." The art that is emerging from L.A.'s nightmare is both unnerving and eerily familiar. 15 x 16; mixed media.

2
Rafal Olbinski, illustrator
Judy Garlan, art director
The Atlantic, client

Magazine article on adoption, "Problem Adoptions." 20 x 16; acrylic on canvas.

3
Russ Willms, illustrator
Anne Wholf, art director
Palm Beach Life, client

Article concerning how the media is attracted to sex scandals, "The Trouble With Paradise." 14 x 20; watercolor.

1

2

PRESS
SEX
WILLMS

1

2

3

4

## Editorial

1 (series)
Mark Summers, illustrator
Alisann Marshall, art director
American Way, American Airlines, design/client

The great grandson of a sea faring family reminisces about sailing, "Go to the Widow-Maker." 6 x 8; scratchboard and watercolor.

2
Steve Kropp, illustrator/designer
Elbert Peck, art director
Sunstone, client

A magazine short story about a woman who wears controversial buttons to church, "Buttons, or Her Strength is in Her Principles." 9¾ x 7; oil, ink, color pencil.

3
Skip Liepke, illustrator
Fred Woodward, art director
Fred Woodward/Gail Anderson/Debra Bishop/Cathy Gilmore-Barnes/Angela Skouras/Geraldine Hessler, designers
Rolling Stone, client

Portrait of Bob Dylan for the 25th anniversary issue of the magazine. 16 x 20; oil.

4
Jeff Koegel, illustrator
David Barnett, art director
Barnett Design Group, design firm
Shearson Lehman Brothers, client

Newsletter cover addresses the company's focus on investment research and evaluation. 11 x 17; acrylic.

## EDITORIAL

1
Mirko Ilić, illustrator
Walter Bernard/Milton Glaser, art directors
Milton Glaser, designer
WBMG, Inc., design firm
International Typeface Corporation, client

Trade magazine, *U&lc*, illustration to explain the origins of the letterform "R." 12 x 17; scratchboard.

2
Albert Rocarols, illustrator
Pablo Dobner, art director
Vivir en Barcelona, client

One of a series of twelve interpretations of the Olympic Games. 7 x 8½; scratchboard and watercolor.

3
Pol Turgeon, illustrator
Catherine Goard, art director
Mary Peligra, designer
Occupational Health & Safety, client

Magazine cover illustration for an article on nursing hazards. 12¾ x 12¾; ink, gouache, varnish.

4
Jack Unruh, illustrator
Fred Woodward, art director
Rolling Stone, client

"An Outlaw at Twilight," movie review of *Unforgiven* starring and directed by Clint Eastwood. 10 x 14; ink and watercolor.

1

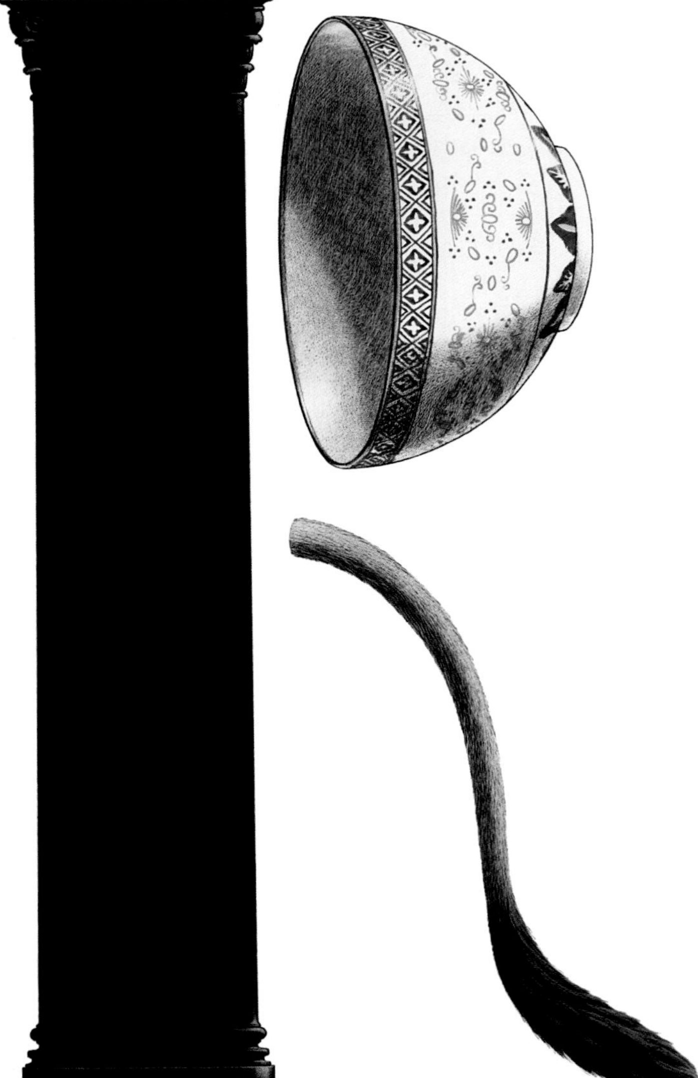

2

3

4

1

2

3

4

## Editorial

1
Nanette Biers, illustrator
Mike Powers, art director
Condé Nast Traveler, client

"Long Weekend" column features an inn each month, this one is Shelter Harbor Inn. 20 x 14; oil on canvas.

2
Gary Baseman, illustrator
Carol Layton, art director
Kelly McMurray, designer
Worth, client

Magazine article about life's frustrations, "Howl." 10½ x 12; pastels.

3
José Ortega, illustrator
Jessica Helfand, art director/designer
Philadelphia Inquirer, client

Article about a Mexican family coming to the United States, "Trapped in the Land of the Free." 10 x 12; pencil, copier, cut paper.

4
Mark Summers, illustrator
Steven Heller, art director
The New York Times Book Review, client

"From Waterloo to Watermelon," reviews of two new books *The Death of Napoleon* and *The Emperor's Last Island*. 8 x 12; scratchboard.

1

2

## EDITORIAL

1
Mary GrandPré, illustrator
Randi Bartsch, art director/designer
Vim & Vigor, client

Magazine article, "An Open Window." Mammography helps women take responsibility for their health. 18 x 24; pastel on paper.

2
Braldt Bralds, illustrator
Fred Woodward, art director
Fred Woodward/Gail Anderson/Debra Bishop/Cathy Gilmore-Barnes/Angela Skouras/Geraldine Hessler, designers
Rolling Stone, client

Portrait of John Lennon for 25th anniversary issue of the magazine. 9½ x 11½; oil on Masonite.

3 (series)
C.F. Payne, illustrator
Fred Woodward, art director
Fred Woodward/Gail Anderson/Debra Bishop/Cathy Gilmore-Barnes/Angela Skouras/Geraldine Hessler, designers
Rolling Stone, client

Portraits of Bruce Springsteen for the 25th anniversary issue of the magazine. 13 x 15½; oil, acrylic, pencil, ink, airbrush, watercolor.

3

## Editorial

1 (series)
William Bramhall, illustrator
Rhonda Rubinstein, art director
Esquire, client

Title of the article, "Notes on the Life & Death and Incandescent Banality of Rock 'N' Roll." Various sizes; pen and ink.

2
Keith Graves, illustrator
J Porter, art director
Yankee Magazine, client

"Father of the Year." Pedro the bull impregnated 75 cows in 45 days. 8 x $9\frac{3}{8}$; Prismacolor and watercolor.

3
Glynis Sweeny, illustrator/designer
Wes Bausmith, art director
The Detroit News, client

Portrait of Ringo Starr. 8 x 12; Prismacolor and pencil.

4
Terry Allen, illustrator
David Armario, art director/designer
Stanford Medicine, client

Office of Communications magazine article, "Peptic Ulcers Revisited." 11 x 14; airbrush.

1

2

3

4

## Editorial

1
Philip Burke, illustrator
Kelly McMurray, art director
Worth, client

Magazine illustration of Salman Rushdie in Note Worthies column. 30 x 40; oil on canvas.

2
Mark English, illustrator
Fred Woodward, art director
Fred Woodward/Gail Anderson/Debra Bishop/Cathy Gilmore-Barnes/Angela Skouras/Geraldine Hessler, designers
Rolling Stone, client

Portrait of Pete Townshend for the 25th anniversary issue of the magazine. 17 x 20; oil and crayon on paper.

## Institutional

3
Daniel Craig, illustrator
Paul Shupanitz, art director
Sietsma K and H Advertising, ad agency
Heartland Bank, client

Christmas card. 14 x 9; acrylic and oil.

4
John Craig, illustrator
Arlene Finger, designer
Finger Smith, design firm
Tri Valley Growers, client

Annual report illustration to show responsibility. 14 x 10; collage and overlays.

1

2

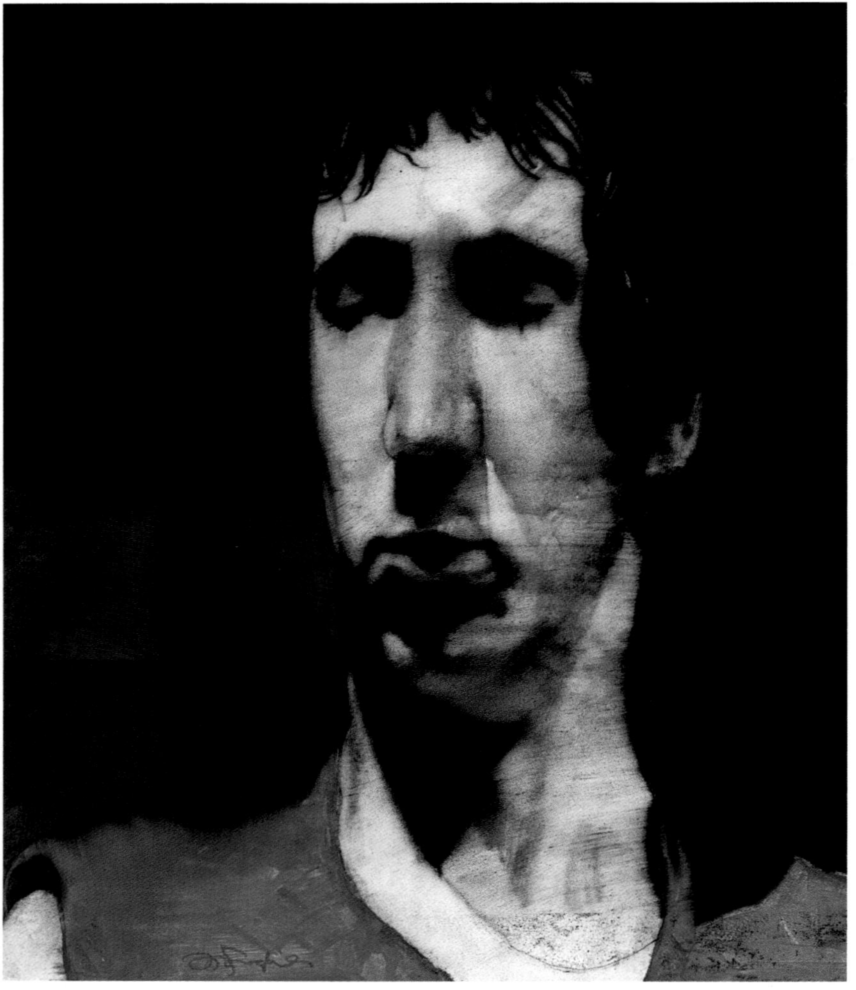

3

4

## INSTITUTIONAL

1 (series)
Jack Unruh, illustrator
Chris Hill, designer
Hill/A Marketing Design Group, design firm
ITESM Campus Monterrey, client

Book given as a gift to commemorate the 75th anniversary of the Mexican school and the 400th anniversary of Cervantes. 9 x 14; ink and watercolor.

1

1

2

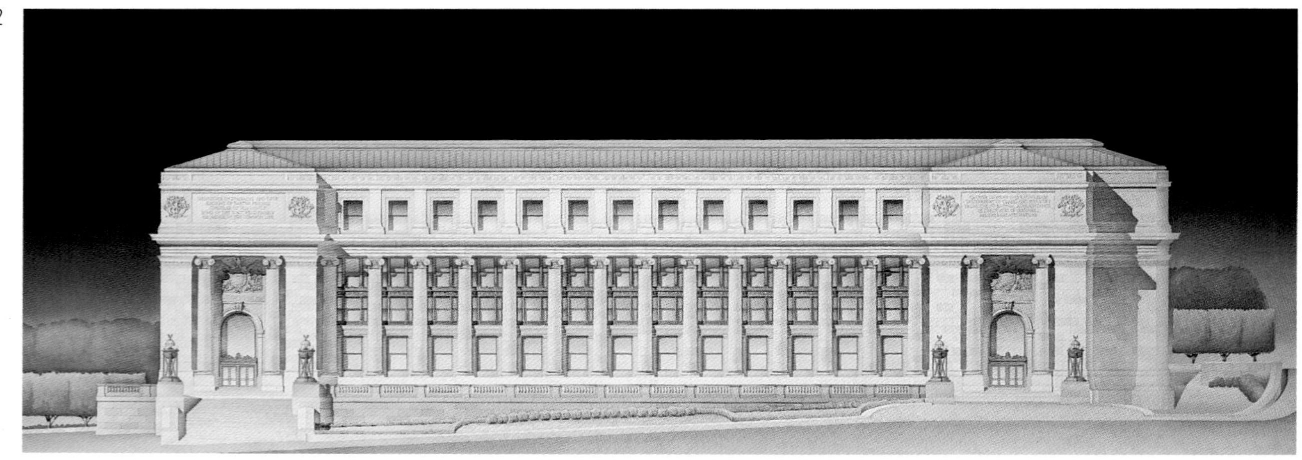

3

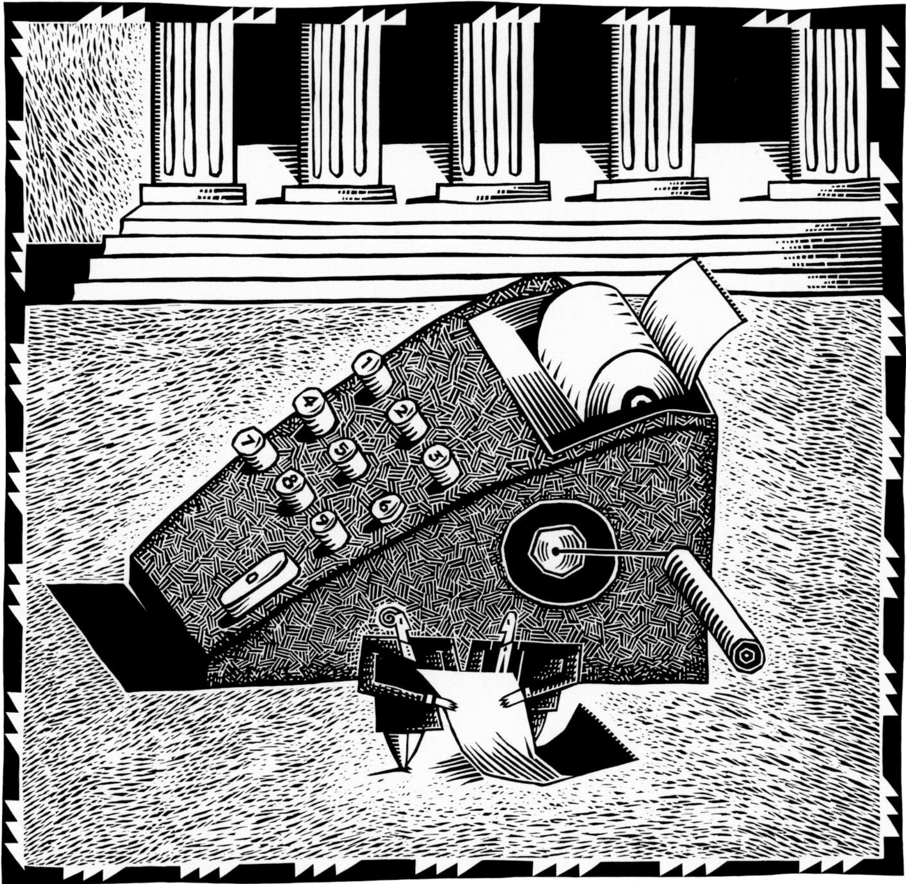

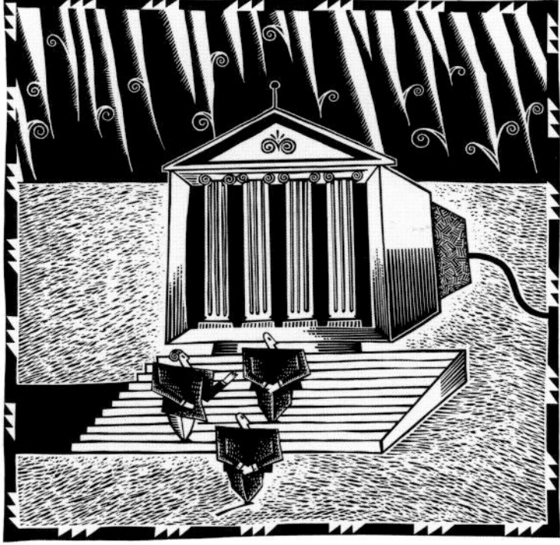

## Institutional

1
John Sposato, illustrator
Anthony Ranieri, art director
John Sposato Design & Illustration, design firm
Macy's, client

Environmental conference. 12 x 12; oil pastel.

2
David M. Genther, illustrator
Lana Rigsby, art director
Lana Rigsby/Troy Ford, designers
Rigsby Design, Inc., design firm
Hines Interests Limited Partnership, client

Poster for historic Washington, D.C., building, Postal Square. 37 x 21½; pencil drawing with an ink wash.

3 (series)
Darrel Kolosta, illustrator
Deborah Berry, designer
Deborah Berry Design, design firm
Cunningham Communications Inc., client

Corporate brochure for publicity firm specializing in high tech companies. 11 x 11; scratchboard.

1

## Institutional

1 (series)
Chris Sheban, illustrator
Mark Oldach, art director
Don Emery, designer
Mark Oldach Design, design firm
Hewitt Associates, client

Employee information brochure illustrations. Eggs: Theme relates to diversification of funds for employee investing program. Clock: You can weather short-term volatility in your investments if you focus on their long-term results. Accepting some volatility now could make a big difference over time. Steps: New funds for employee investing, each slightly higher than the previous one on a risk/return scale. 9 x 11; watercolor, pencil, pastel.

## INSTITUTIONAL

1

1 (series)
René Milot, illustrator
Jean-Pierre Veilleux/Robert Boulay, art directors
Irvin Lebovits, creative director
The Gingko Group Ltd., design firm
Stentor, client

Telecommunications company mailer resembling baseball cards. Various sizes; oil on canvas.

## Institutional

1
Linda Bleck, illustrator
Cynthia Kampf, art director/designer
Tripp Design, design firm
Imcera Group Inc., client

Call for entries to promote waste reduction. 7 x 7; gouache.

2 (series)
John English, illustrator
Mark J. Spencer, art director
David Westbrook, designer
Corporate Communications Group Inc., design
Yellow Freight System Inc., client

The series illustrates Poetry in Motion. "The House by the Side of the Road" by Sam Walter Foss; "Fog" by Carl Sandburg; and "Song of the Open Road" by Walt Whitman. 36 x 24; oil on canvas.

1

2

## Institutional

1
Philippe Lardy, illustrator
Alison K. Grevstad, art director
Nordstrom, design/client

Cover for in-house booklet. Subject: Wise.
Watercolor, ink.

2 (series)
John Craig, illustrator
Gordon Mortensen, art director/designer
Cavalli & Cribbs, ad agency
Mortensen Design, design firm
Stanford University, client

14 x 11; collage and overlays; collage, ink, scratchboard; collage.

1

2

SAT SUN MON TUE
RAIN RAIN

## Institutional

1
René Milot, illustrator
Nanistya Martohardjono, art director
Spencer Francey Peters, design firm
National Ballet of Canada, client

Invitation card for *The Taming of the Shrew.* 11 x 20; oil on canvas.

2
Leland Burke, illustrator
Ted Fabella, art director/designer
Atlanta Botanical Garden, client

Annual report. "Gardening Techniques" written by Lisa Frank. 11 x 10; pen and ink.

3
Larry McEntire, illustrator
Gary Easterly, art director
Jacqueline Brunner, designer
Easterly & Company, design firm
Pueblo-to-People, client

Catalog cover and T-shirt art for import company. 7 x 9 1/2; watercolor.

4
John Mattos, illustrator
Stephen Martin, art director
Mary Boyer, designer
Corporate Graphics, design firm
Kaufman & Broad, client

Cover for residential housing developer's annual report. 9 x 12; airbrush and ink.

1

2

3

4

1

2

## INSTITUTIONAL

1
R.M. Kato, illustrator
Fred Fehlau, art director
Four Way Communications, publisher
Playboy Jazz Festival, client

Portrait of Billy Cobham for the program. $10^1/_4$ x $12^1/_2$; gouache.

2 (series)
Jon Flaming, illustrator/designer
Ron Sullivan, art director
SullivanPerkins, design firm
GTE Directories Corporation, client

$8^1/_2$ x 11; cut amber and ink on paper.

1

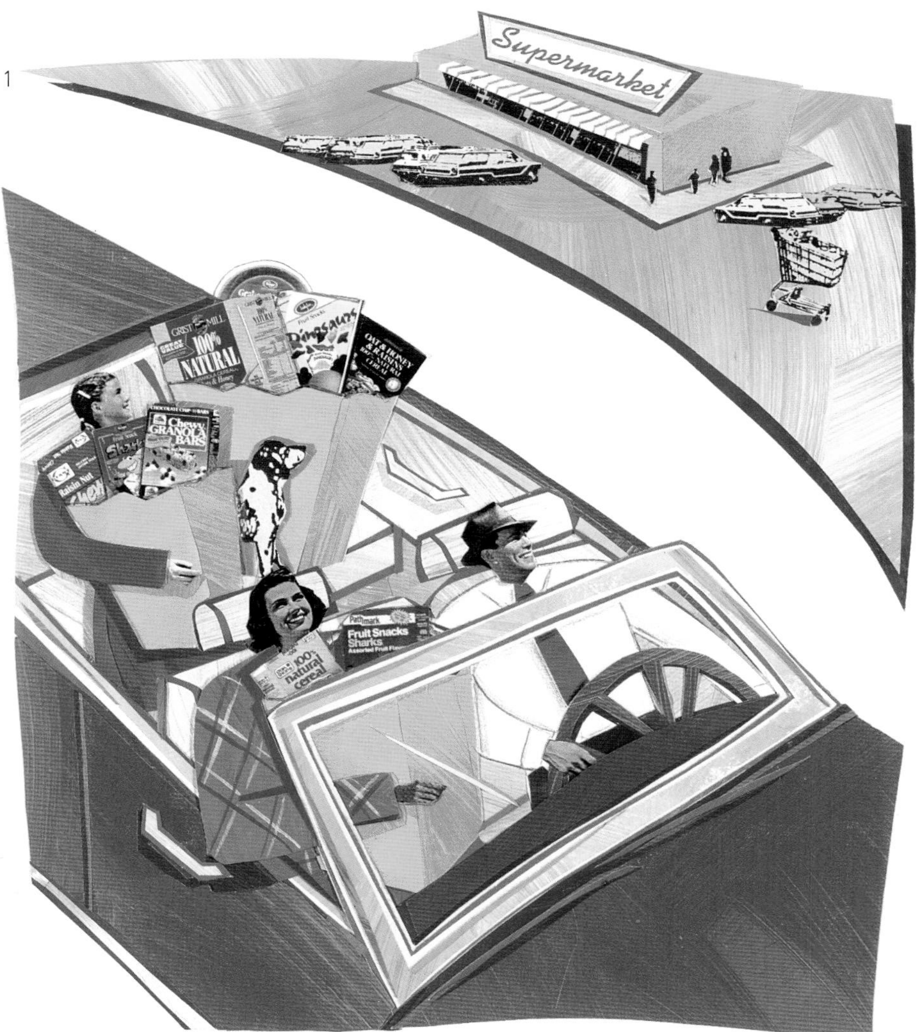


## INSTITUTIONAL

1 (series)
Tom Garrett, illustrator
Nancy Grunthaner, art director
Jim Nancekivell/Nancy Grunthaner, designers
The Nancekivell Group, design firm
Grist Mill Co., client

Annual report. 16 x 20; collage.

2
Tom Curry, illustrator
Peter Deutsch, art director/designer
Deutsch Design, design firm
Center for Global Partnership, client

Annual report. 14 x 14; acrylic on hardboard.

2

1

INSTITUTIONAL

1 (series)
Ward Schumaker, illustrator/designer
Schumaker, design firm
Moose's, client

Restaurant illustrations for coffee menu, stationery, press folder, neon sign, direct mail, etc. Various sizes; pen and ink.

2
Nicholas Wilton, illustrator
Arlene Finger, art director/designer
Finger and Smith Design, design firm
Tri Valley Growers, client

Annual report illustrating the idea of improvement. 8 x 8; acrylic.

2

## SELF-PROMOTION

1
Tracy Sabin, illustrator
Lisa Porter, art director/designer
Design Safari, design firm
Icarus Studio, client

Brochure illustration for a hand-made paper company.
9 x 15 3/4; mechanical separations.

2
Etienne Delessert, illustrator
Rita Marshall, art director
Delessert & Marshall, design firm
Musée des Arts Décoratifs/UQAM Design Center, clients

Poster for Delessert retrospective tour.
6 x 7; watercolor.

3 (series)
Anthony Chiappin, illustrator/designer
Shayne Pooley, art director
Benchmark Advertising, ad agency/client

Promotional booklet. 10 3/4 x 15 1/2; acrylic.

1

2

3

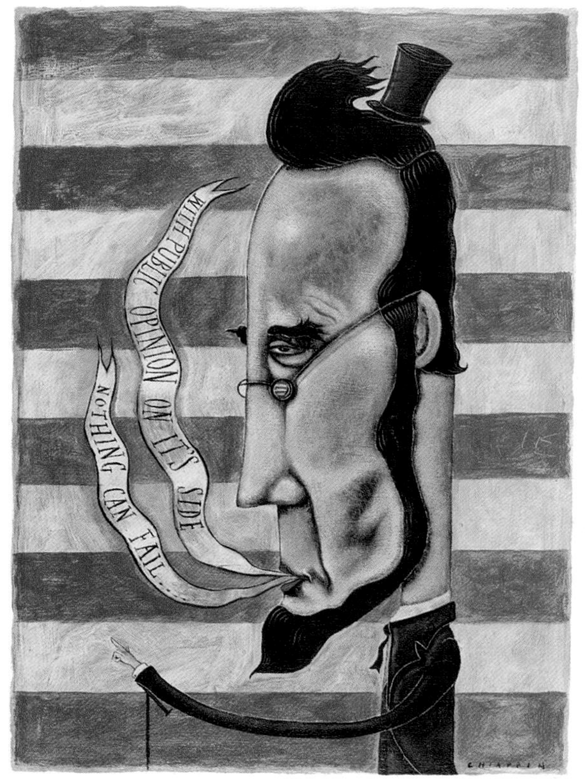
WITH PUBLIC OPINION ON IT'S SIDE
NOTHING CAN FAIL...

READY, FIRE, AIM

BRAND X
Brand X
Brand X

1

2

## Self-Promotion

1
Alex Murawski, illustrator/client
Akiva Boker, art director
Blue Brick Design, design firm
Lasky Printers, client

Calendar. 16 x 16; ink and cell vinyl.

2 (series)
Craig Frazier, illustrator/art director/designer
Frazier Design, design firm/client

Promotional booklet. Various sizes; cut paper.

## Self-Promotion

1
Raphael Montoliu, illustrator
Paul Browning, art director
John Sheng/Peter Baker, designers
Taylor & Browning Design Associates, design firm
Art Directors Club of Toronto, client

Cover of the call for entries competition. 12 x 17; pen and ink, airbrush.

2
Bill Mayer, illustrator
Alan Lidji, art director/designer
Lidji Design, design firm
Williamson Printing, client

Poster, "For You and Your Big Ideas." 18½ x 25; airbrush, gouache, dye.

3
Cheryl Chalmers, illustrator/client

Mailer. 15½ x 20½; watercolor.

3

## SELF-PROMOTION

1 (series)
Frank Viva, illustrator/art director/designer
Frank Viva/Doug Dolan, creative directors
Viva Dolan Communications & Design, design firm
Arjo Wiggins Fine Papers Ltd., client

Pocket cards used as give-aways and printed as add-ons when a larger job is in production. 3½ x 5; chalk and watercolor.

2
Mike Reagan, illustrator/art director/designer/client

Mailer. 21 x 22; watercolor, ink, coffee.

1

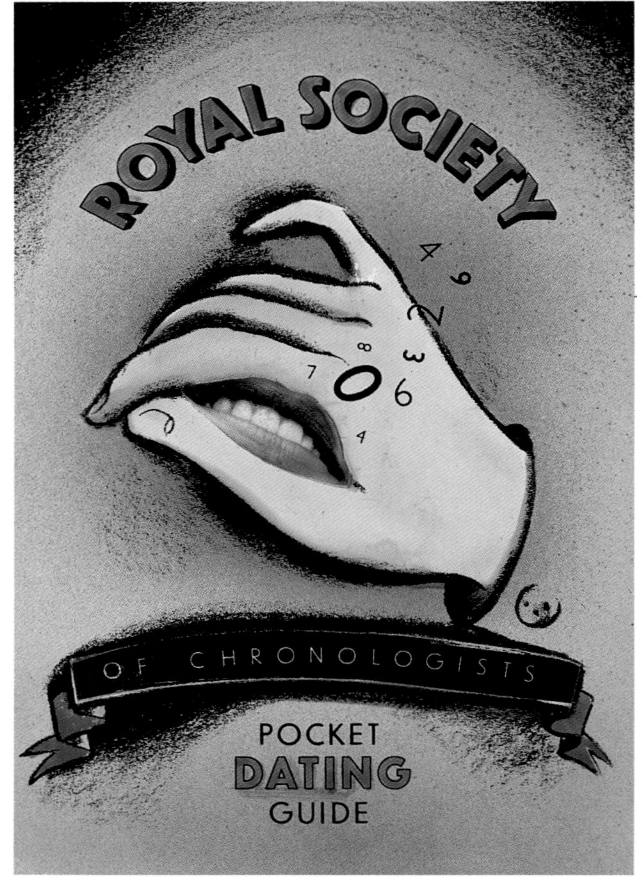

1

2

## Self-Promotion

1
Anita Kunz, illustrator
Bob Hambly, art director/designer
Hambly & Woolley Design, design firm
Grenville Press, client

Printing company greeting card. 24 x 36; watercolor and gouache.

2
Philippe Lardy, illustrator

Mailer.

3
Bill Mayer, illustrator
Don Smith, art director
Kirk Smith, designer
The Adsmith, ad agency
Hopper Paper, client

Poster. 10 x 14; airbrush, gouache, dye, stripped-in color.

3

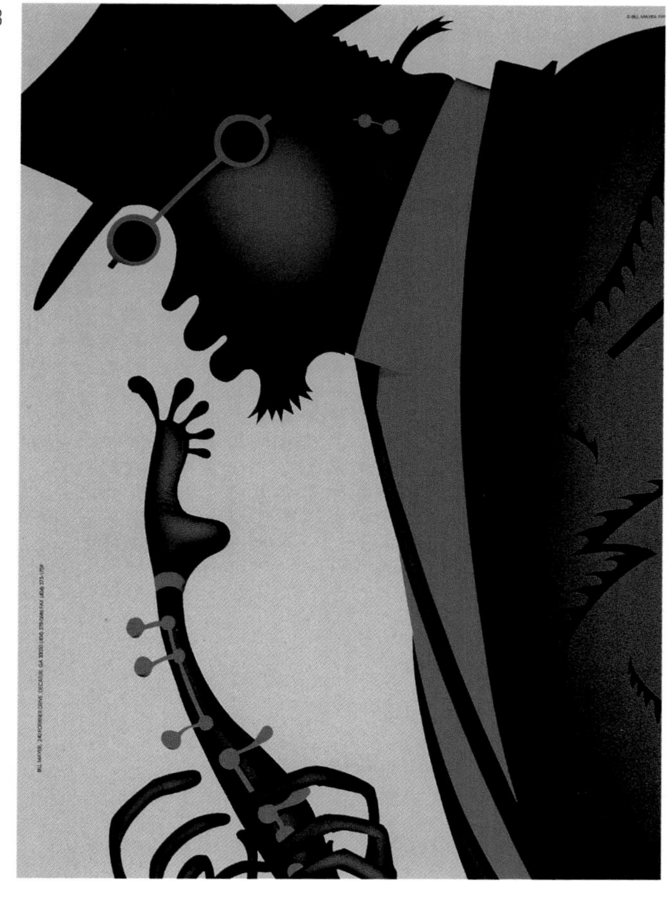

1

2

3

## SELF-PROMOTION

1
Erik Drageset, illustrator/art director/designer/client

Mailer. 22 x 14; charcoal.

2
Joseph Lorusso, illustrator/client

Mailer. 14 x 11; oil.

3
Bob Conge, illustrator/art director/designer/client

Ad. 18 x 24; sepia ink line and watercolor.

4
Don Arday, illustrator
Don Arday, Photocom Inc., client

Postcard mailer. 5 x 7; electronic illustration.

4

## Unpublished

1
Ellen Suh, illustrator
David Mocarsky, art director

*Yellow Wallpaper* book cover. 10 x 16; acrylic.

© Ellen Suh 1993

2
Andrea Ventura, illustrator
Achille Villa, art director/designer

Record jacket. 13 x 14 1/2; charcoal and gesso.

© Andrea Ventura 1993

3
Tim Lewis, illustrator/art director

5 1/2 x 6; watercolor on Xeroxed watercolor paper.

© Tim Lewis 1993

4 (series)
Jody Hewgill, illustrator
Jody Hewgill/Kim Yokota, art directors
Shikatani LaCroix Inc., design firm
Brewer's Retail Stores, client

Pediment murals. Various sizes; acrylic.

© Jody Hewgill 1993

1

2

3

4

1

2

3

4

5

## UNPUBLISHED

1
Ronald Slabbers, illustrator/designer
Marcel Rotteveel, art director

Illustration for an article about sexual harassment for a new magazine that never got off the ground. 11¾ x 14½; gouache on cardboard.

© Ronald Slabbers 1993

2
Pascal Milelli, illustrator

Portfolio piece. 18 x 22; oil on paper.

© Pascal Milelli 1993

3
Karen Chandler, illustrator/art director

42 x 35; oil on board.

© Karen Chandler 1993

4
Irena Roman, illustrator

Portfolio piece. 12 x 16; watercolor.

© Irena Roman 1993

5
Steve Miller, illustrator/art director

5¾ x 9; oil pastel.

© Steve Miller 1993

1

2

## Unpublished

1
Gary Head, illustrator

Portfolio piece. 10 x 8; oil.

© Gary Head 1993

2 (series)
Eric Masi, illustrator

Various sizes; acrylic and gouache on canvas.

© Eric Masi 1993

## Unpublished

1
Don Asmussen, illustrator/art director/designer

14 x 22; pen and ink, watercolor and collage.

© Don Asmussen 1993

2
Irene Rofheart-Pigott, illustrator

Portfolio piece. 11 x 14; oil on paper.

© Irene Rofheart-Pigott 1993

3
Don Arday, illustrator
Don Arday, Photocom Inc., client

5 x 7; electronic illustration.

© Don Arday 1993

4
Will Williams, illustrator/art director
Wood Ronsaville Harlin, Inc., design firm

34 x 51; oil.

© Will Williams 1993

1

2

3

4

## UNPUBLISHED

1
Eric Hanson, illustrator/art director

$8\frac{1}{2} \times 8\frac{3}{4}$; ink and watercolor.

© Eric Hanson 1993

2 (series)
Barry E. Jackson, illustrator/art director

Concept illustrations for Cool World Productions, Paramount Pictures. Various sizes; acrylic.

© Barry E. Jackson 1993

1

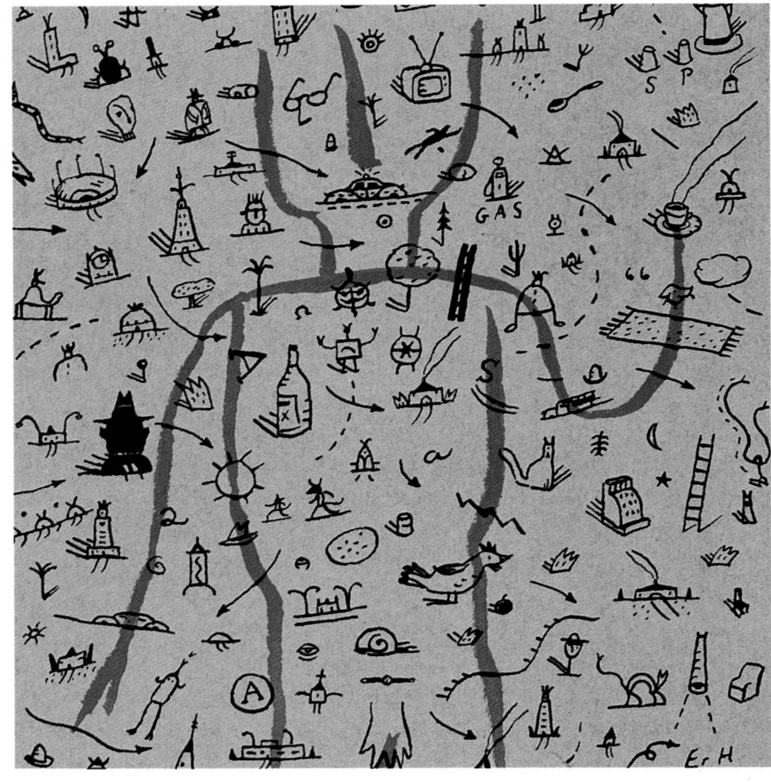


2

## Unpublished

1
Mathew McFarren, illustrator/art director

Portrait of the artist's cat, Kate. 18 x 24; oil.

© Mathew McFarren 1993

2
Albert Rocarols, illustrator/art director

Painting for an exhibition. 19¾ x 27½; acrylic on paper.

© Albert Rocarols 1993

1

2

# INDEX

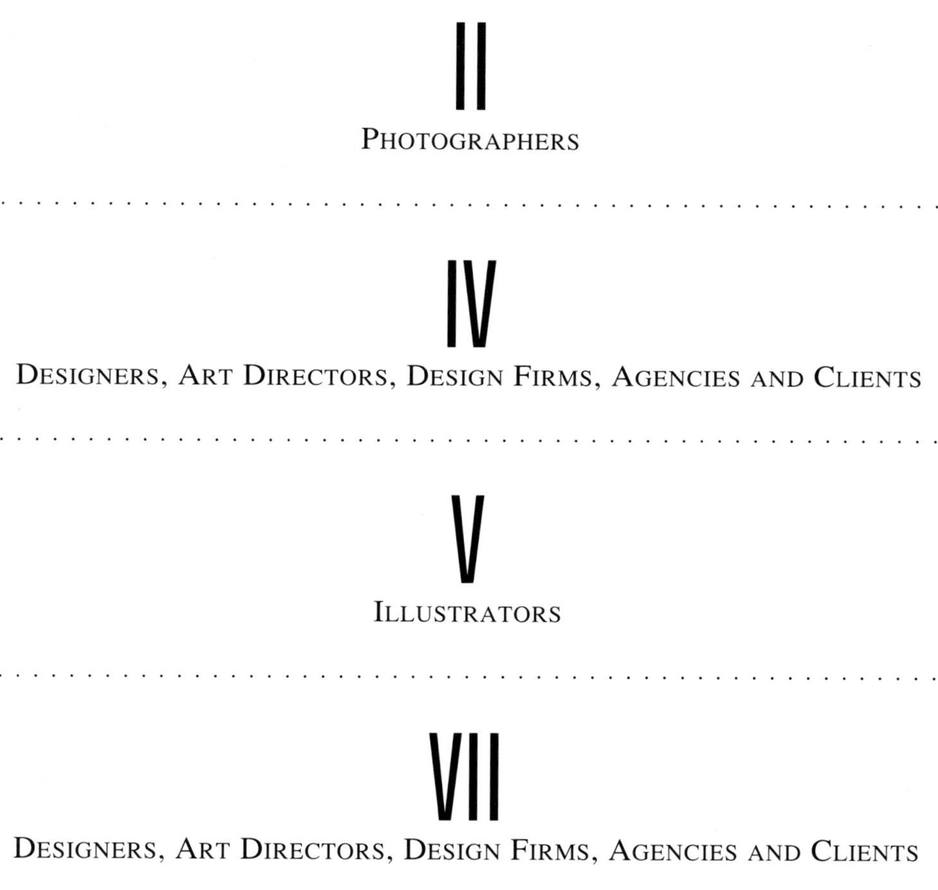

## II

PHOTOGRAPHERS

## IV

DESIGNERS, ART DIRECTORS, DESIGN FIRMS, AGENCIES AND CLIENTS

## V

ILLUSTRATORS

## VII

DESIGNERS, ART DIRECTORS, DESIGN FIRMS, AGENCIES AND CLIENTS

# Index to Photographers

**Mark, Mary Ellen** 59, 68
Phone (212) 925-2770
134 Spring Street, Suite 502
New York, NY 10012

**Marsico, Dennis** 66, 78
Phone (412) 781-6349
110 Fahnestock Road
Pittsburgh, PA 15215

**McArthur, Pete** 41, 71
Phone (310) 815-1951
8741 W. Washington Boulevard, Suite A
Culver City, CA 90232

**McLeod, William Mercer** 129
Phone (415) 550-7576
225 Fair Oaks Street
San Francisco, CA 94110

**McSpadden, Wyatt** 37
Phone (512) 322-9102
P.O. Box 650098
Austin, TX 78765

**Meeks, Raymond** 53
Phone (617) 643-6022
21 Pine Street
Arlington, MA 02174

**Michl, Joe** 112
Phone (612) 874-1999
Parallel Productions
2010 1st Avenue S.
Minneapolis, MN 55404

**Miles, Bill** 13
Phone (617) 426-6862
374 Congress Street, Suite 304
Boston, MA 02210

**Miller, Dennis** 110
Phone (310) 546-3205
1467 12th Street, #C
Manhattan Beach, CA 90266

**Mizono, Robert** 10
Phone (415) 648-3993
650 Alabama Street, #301
San Francisco, CA 94110

**Murphy, Dennis** 6
Phone (214) 651-7516
101 Howell
Dallas, TX 75207

## N

**Nachoum, Amos** 77
Phone (212) 877-9251
42 W. 87th Street
New York, NY 10024

**Neleman, Hans** 9
Phone (212) 274-1000
77 Mercer Street
New York, NY 10012

**Niedorf, Steve** 95
Phone (612) 332-7124
700 Washington Avenue N., #304
Minneapolis, MN 55401

**Nielsen, Ed** 84
Phone (415) 853-4136
2650 S. Bert Crane Road
Atwater, CA 95301

**Nolton, Gary** 99
Phone (503) 228-0844
Nolton Studio
107 N.W. Fifth Avenue
Portland, OR 97209

**Norberg, Marc** 103
Phone (612) 340-9863
25 N. 4th Street, 4th Floor
Minneapolis, MN 55401

## O

**O'Brien, Michael** 16, 138
Phone (800) 597-7511
6502 Minikahda Cove
Austin, TX 78746

**O'Rear, Charles** 83
Phone (707) 963-2663
2140 Dean York Lane
St. Helena, CA 94574

**Ott, Jeff** 22
Phone (214) 638-0602
2328 Farrington
Dallas, TX 75207

## P

**Payne, Steve** 63
Phone (416) 778-9504
58 Denison Avenue
Toronto, Ontario M5T 2M8
Canada

**Peebles, Daniel** 141
Phone (602) 622-7133
Swanstock
P.O. Box 2350
Tucson, AZ 85702

**Peters, Tim** 63
Phone (716) 283-6019
P.O. Box 404
Buffalo, NY 14205

**Peterson, Bryan F.** 6
Phone (503) 227-5948
1125 N.W. 16th
Portland, OR 97209

**Pickett, Keri** 50
Phone (612) 339-0460
17 Greenway Gables
Minneapolis, MN 55403

## R

**Rigau, Felix** 91
Phone (415) 928-1933
3035 Baker Street, #103
San Francisco, CA 94123

**Robbins, Bill** 27
Phone (310) 314-7771
228 Main Street
Venice, CA 90291

**Ross, Alan** 146
Phone (415) 495-1900
123 S. Park Street
San Francisco, CA 94107

**Rusing, Rick** 9
Phone (602) 967-1864
1555 W. University, #106
Tempe, AZ 85281

**Ryan, Tom** 31, 37
Phone (214) 651-7085
2919 Canton
Dallas, TX 75226

## S

**Sacha, Bob** 59
Phone (212) 749-4128
12 W. 96th Street, #14B
New York, NY 10025

**Schatz, Howard** 45
Phone (415) 457-0810
P.O. Box 640350
San Francisco, CA 94164

**Scherer, Jim** 119
Phone (617) 338-5678
35 Kingston Street
Boston, MA 02111

**Schleipman, Russ** 105
Phone (617) 267-1677
298 A Columbus Avenue
Boston, MA 02116

**Schnepf, James** 32
Phone (414) 691-3980
W277 N2730 Trillium Lane
Pewaukee, WI 53072

**Schneps, Michael** 144
Phone (415) 821-4845
4104 24th Street, #352
San Francisco, CA 94114

**Schulman, Scott C.** 92
Phone (310) 306-2191
4311 Lyceum Avenue
Los Angeles, CA 90066

**Schwarm, Brad** 9
Phone (307) 733-5353
P.O. Box 2962
Jackson, WY 83001

**Sedlik, Jeff** 42
Phone (213) 626-3323
940 E. Second Street, Studio 8
Los Angeles, CA 90012

**Seliger, Mark** 64, 83
Phone (212) 941-6548
96 Grand Street, #3F
New York, NY 10013

**Shafer, Dave** 120
Phone (404) 876-1992
1579 Monroe Drive, Suite 156
Atlanta, GA 30324

**Sharpe, Scott** 48
Phone (919) 829-4735
The News & Observer Photo Department
215 S. McDowell Street
Raleigh, NC 27602

**Shimlock, Maurine** 91
Phone (512) 328-1201
P.O. Box 162931
Austin, TX 78716

**Shinn, Chris** 81, 91
Phone (713) 526-2623
2411 Bartlett
Houston, TX 77098

**Shoemake, Allan Hunter** 144
Phone (201) 467-4920
56 Main Street
Millburn, NJ 07041

**Sinkler, Paul** 115
Phone (612) 343-0325
420 N. 5th Street, #516
Minneapolis, MN 55401

**Smale, Brian** 71
Phone (212) 627-4687
251 W. 19th Street, #1C
New York, NY 10011

**Smith, Ron Baxter** 136
Phone (416) 462-3040
11 Carlaw Avenue, Unit 4
Toronto, Ontario M4M 2R6
Canada

**Spalding, Clem** 131
Phone (210) 271-7273
107 Blue Star
San Antonio, TX 78204

**Springmann, Christopher** 72
Phone (415) 663-8428
P.O. Box 745
Pt. Reyes, CA 94956

**Staller, Jan** 71
Phone (212) 219-1048
37 Walker Street
New York, NY 10013

**Stevens, Bob** 146
Phone (310) 822-0121
1800-A Abbot Kinney Boulevard
Venice, CA 90291

**Stoecklein, Dave** 131
Phone (208) 726-5191
P.O. Box 856
Ketchum, ID 83340

## T

**Tejada, David X.** 106
Phone (303) 979-0171
12036 W. Brandt Place
Denver, CO 80127

**Thain, Alastair** 75
Phone (310) 278-7163
614 N. Beverly Drive
Beverly Hills, CA 90210

**Thompson, William** 133
Phone (206) 621-9069
15566 Sandy Hook Road
Poulsbo, WA 98370

**Toerge, David G.** 48
Phone (415) 824-7099
3972 Folsom Street
San Francisco, CA 94110

**Topelmann, Lars** 31
Phone (503) 224-4556
1314 N.W. Irving, #214
Portland, OR 97209

**Trent, Brad** 35
Phone (212) 627-2147
666 Greenwich Street
New York, NY 10014

**Turner, Danny** 68, 77
Phone (214) 826-1130
4228 Main Street
Dallas, TX 75226

**Turner, Pete** 115
Phone (516) 537-2434
P.O. Box 203
Wainscott, NY 11973

**Varde, Abhijit** 97
Phone (415) 928-8039
840 Taylor Street, #4
San Francisco, CA 94108

**Vedros, Nick** 13
Phone (816) 471-5488
Vedros & Associates
215 W. 19th Street
Kansas City, MO 64108

**Venville, Malcolm** 22
Phone (44) 71-436-5191
23 Nassau Street, Basement
London W1N 7RF
England

## W

**Wade, Chriss** 54
Phone (212) 795-8764
615 Fort Washington Avenue
New York, NY 10040

**Walsh, Frank** 24
Phone (412) 621-1268
Rieder & Walsh Photography
424 N. Craig Street
Pittsburgh, PA 15213

**Wells, Heidi Kirsten** 63
Phone (617) 232-7417
1284 Beacon Street, Suite 610
Brookline, MA 02146

**Westmoreland, Graham** 22, 31
Phone (44) 9-24276493
18 Carr Lane
Middlestown, Wakefield
W. Yorks WF4 4QJ
England

**Wexler, Glen** 16, 143
Phone (213) 465-0268
736 N. Highland Avenue
Los Angeles, CA 90038

**Wilkes, Stephen** 31
Phone (212) 475-4010
48 E. 13th Street
New York, NY 10003

**Winters, Dan** 84
Phone (213) 874-1949
6383 Bryn Mawr Drive
Los Angeles, CA 90068

**Woodward, Fred** 41
Phone (212) 484-1655
Rolling Stone
1290 Avenue of the Americas
New York, NY 10104

**Wreszin, Daniel** 9
Phone (213) 937-3021
437 N. Sycamore, Suite 204
Los Angeles, CA 90036

**Xu, Jiashu** 61
Phone (61) 8-346-5683
34 Belford Avenue
Devon Park SA 5008
Australia

**Editor's Note**

Every effort has been made to ensure that the credits comply with information supplied to us.

# INDEX TO DESIGNERS, ART DIRECTORS, DESIGN FIRMS, AGENCIES AND CLIENTS

**Editor's Note**

Every effort has been made to ensure that the credits comply with information supplied to us.

# Index to Illustrators

**Editor's Note**

Every effort has been made to ensure that the credits comply with information supplied to us.

# INDEX TO DESIGNERS, ART DIRECTORS, DESIGN FIRMS, AGENCIES AND CLIENTS

## Index to Designers, Art Directors, Design Firms, Agencies and Clients.



**Editor's Note**

Every effort has been made to ensure that the credits comply with information supplied to us.